ROSES

Nancy Gardiner
and
Peter Harkness

ROSES

Nancy Gardiner
and
Peter Harkness

NEW
HOLLAND

First published in the UK in 1993 by
New Holland (Publishers) Ltd
37 Connaught Street, London W2 2AZ

ISBN 1 85368 192 X

Editor: Sean Fraser
Designer: Tracey Carstens
Cover designer: Tracey Carstens
Illustrator: Nicci Page
Sepia photographs: David Bennett and Jeremy Gibbon
Typeset by Diatype Setting CC
Originated by Unifoto (Pty) Ltd
Printed and bound in Singapore by Kyodo Printing Co (Pte) Ltd

CONTENTS

ACKNOWLEDGEMENTS

I am most grateful to those many gardeners, too many to mention, who so generously shared their beautiful roses with me, and allowed me to photograph them. Gillian and Taffy Walters willingly picked armfuls of roses from their flower farm, and Rose van Staden constantly kept me updated with news of her old roses as they bloomed, as did Fay and John Clayton. Lynn Keppler, too, lovingly shared her vast store of knowledge, and her abiding love of roses. I would also like to thank Joan Pinnell and Dawn Pellew, who helped with the roses and the arrangements; and Ludwig Taschner, leading rose nurseryman, of Ludwig's Roses, who kindly agreed to check the manuscript. A special word of thanks must indeed go to my co-author, Peter Harkness, internationally acclaimed rose expert, who generously gave of his time to evaluate and refine the original text.

To create the cameo pictures in this book, I was most fortunate to have been lent a number of beautiful heirlooms by Frances and David Bradford, Ann Denny, Lorraine Kettley and Jean Mitchell. The latter three, together with Joan Wright, also happily helped in the setting up of these pictures, as well as contributing a bounty of roses used in the artistic arrangements. A final thank you to the entire team who helped put this book together, especially to the editor, Sean Fraser, and designer, Tracey Carstens, for their invaluable time and effort. The making of this book, although it has involved a great deal of work, has been a happy experience indeed, with the love of roses inspiring every encounter, and I am deeply grateful for having been given this unique opportunity of looking into every enchanting aspect of this glorious and well-loved flower.

Nancy Gardiner

NANCY GARDINER

INTRODUCING THE ROSE

But thou of every flower art Queen;
And who can tell thy royal worth?
For midst the rest, when thou art seen,
Thou reignest o'er the gems of earth.

GEOFFREY HENSLOW

Roses, having found their place and purpose in the pattern of Creation, opened their face to the sun many millions of years before the arrival of Man. When the two came together, there grew between them a special and wonderful relationship which was to last for many centuries to come.

No other flower has given rise to such a wealth of poetry and art, evoked such emotion and romance, or been the subject of so many legends and beliefs. In many lands throughout the world, it became the symbol of love and even of war. The love of roses is recognised among all nations, and all ages. Rich and poor, the academic and illiterate, the countryman and town dweller are all seemingly bewitched by the splendour of the rose.

Those who grow roses have no need to explain their attachment. Their approach is one of simple, wholehearted admiration. For they have entered the magical world of roses, with their awe-inspiring range of colour, shape and fragrance, and even antiquity.

They plant roses when the icy hand of winter is upon the garden, and are blessed with enough imagination to look forward to a season filled with unsurpassable beauty. Those who have never grown a rose may still be stirred by the touching simplicity of a single dog rose, or a full grown voluptuous beauty, resplendent in petals of shining satin. For this is veritably the Queen of Flowers.

What is it that sets the rose apart? Perhaps the following pages may help to solve this enchanting mystery.

THE HISTORY OF THE ROSE

Oh, no man knows
Through what wild centuries
Roves back the rose

WALTER DE LA MARE (1873-1956)

The poet is right – for the very earliest roses are mere fossil fragments which could be up to twenty million years old. These fragments are the forerunners of today's wild rose. They were simple flowers with five petals and enough pollen to ensure that a multitude of seeds could be carried from their Central Asian heartland right across the northern hemisphere, circling the pole from Siberia westwards to Alaska, adapting to the warmth of Arabia and North Africa, sweeping across Europe and extending over North America as far south as Mexico.

New forms arose in response to changes in environment, so that over 100 distinct wild species are found in the world today. Among them *R. pimpinellifolia* (Scotch or Burnet Rose) is one of the most hardy, and *R. bracteata* (Macartney Rose) one of the most beautiful.

In the words of rosarian E. A. Bunyard, 'It might almost be said that the rose is an index of civilisation'. When where roses first cultivated? We read of roses in the Imperial gardens of China as early as the sixth century BC, and it is clear that Chinese roses, together with the much loved peonies and chrysanthemums, were cultivated with reverence and admiration, being painted on porcelain and silk and reproduced in books. Hybrids and improved forms of these ancient roses brought new shapes and colours, and extended their flowering time. Chinese

OLD STONE STEPS LEAD TO A WOODEN ARCH DRAPED
WITH PAUL'S SCARLET.

tion. In 810 AD the Sultan of Baghdad demanded that his Persian subjects should pay him 30,000 bottles of rosewater a year as tribute. Four centuries later, camels were being laden with the precious liquid to cleanse Saladin's mosques after Crusader occupation.

The roses valued for these uses were Gallicas and Damasks. The pinky-red Gallica has an ancient history, and was perhaps known to the Medes and Persians from 1200 BC onwards. Its petals have the rare quality of re-taining and even intensifying their fragrance after dying. Improved full-petalled forms such as 'Officinalis' (which means 'Apothecary's Rose') have long been cultivated, notably at Provins in France. They were used to fill cush-ions and pillows, to make into conserves, and to provide medicine to 'strengthen the heart . . . liver, kidneys and other weake intrails . . . dry and comfort a weake stom-acke that is flashie and moist . . .'. The reputation of this herbal remedy was such that Napoleon is said to have relied on it for the well-being of his troops.

The Damask has a softer texture in its petals which makes it more sweet-smelling than the Gallica, and so more suitable for the process of distillation. It is still being grown commercially today in Bulgaria, Saudi Arabia, Turkey, India and Morocco.

gardeners prized and tended them for centuries. When at last the world discovered these hidden treasures, they caused a revolution in rose growing.

Earlier evidence of roses comes from clay tablets, buried at Ur (Iraq) and dated to 2000 BC. These mention the purchase of rosewater, a commodity for which fields of roses are still grown today. While the Chinese grew roses for their beauty, it seems that they were first cultivat-ed in the western world for their usefulness. There is a simple explanation for this. Western roses had special qualities of fragrance that those of the Orient lacked, making them perfect for cosmetic use and for overriding unpleasant odours. Rosarian G. S. Thomas suggests that in those days rose oil was 'even more valuable than gold'. From Greece we read of Hector's body being bathed in rose oil, and of Sappho and her ladies adorning their per-sons with roses, which they termed 'The Queen of Flow-ers'. The Romans used roses at their feasts to lie on them and be wreathed in them ('to allay the fumes of drunken-ness'), and the crazed Emperor Heliogabalus (204-222 AD) carried the practice of showering rose petals on the guests to new extremes, indeed to the point of suffoca-

A SINGLE ROSE HINTS AT THE NOSTALGIA OF
A FORGOTTEN ERA.

Rosewater in varying strengths is produced from the Damask rose, as well as the very precious attar of roses, a perfume derived from the essential oil of roses. It can take 100,000 blooms to produce an ounce of attar.

Ancient roses and those derived from them are today called Old Garden Roses. As well as Gallicas and Damasks, they include Albas and Centifolias. Alba means 'white' but pink forms certainly do exist, and the group includes the strange 'York and Lancaster' rose which bears flowers of beautifully mixed hues.

Alba roses are tough and so long-lived that a 'Maiden's Blush' established in an Oxfordshire garden has already outstayed several generations of the family, and looks good for years to come. The rich pink Centifolia or 'Hundred Leav'd Rose' is notable for its many petals, and it provides the basis of the rose perfume industry at Grasse in southern France. In England this old fashioned rose is called the 'Cabbage Rose'.

From these four groups – Gallica, Damask, Alba and Centifolia – scores of delightful Old Garden Roses evolved in the centuries up to 1800. A good number have survived. They grow easily, and display their beauty and fragrance through the weeks of summer with flowers of white, purple and many shades of pink. Poets and artists are inspired now, as in past centuries, to portray their loveliness in all kinds of ways – on ceramics, silks, canvas and the printed page.

NEW WORLDS

The earliest printed list of roses grown in England dates from 1596. In it, 16 items are given by John Gerarde, including two recent arrivals from Asia, the vivid 'Austrian Yellow' and the dazzling bright 'Austrian Copper'. These roses are an arresting sight today, and must have been sensational in an age when such colours were a novelty.

More delights were in store as trade routes opened to the east. Chinese roses began arriving in Europe from 1750 onwards. First came the 'Parson's Pink' (or 'Monthly Rose'). It reached England in 1789 and was said to be 'in every cottage garden' by 1823. But what made it so

THE PROLIFIC BLOOMS OF ROSA RUGOSA ADD BRILLIANT
COLOUR TO THE GARDEN.

Eye of the garden, queen of flowers,
Love's cup wherein lie nectar's
*   powers,*
Ingender'd first of nectar:
Sweet nurse-child of the spring's
*   young hours,*
And beauty's fair character.

Bless'd jewel that the earth
*   doth wear,*
E'en when the brave young sun
*   draws near,*
To her hot love pretending:
Himself likewise form doth bear,
At rising and descending.

Rose of the queen of love belov'd:
England's great kings divinely mov'd,
Gave roses in their banner:
It show'd that beauty's rose indeed
Now in this age should them succeed,
And reign in more sweet manner.

SIR JOHN DAVIES

ROSA CENTIFOLIA IS PRESERVED IN FINE DETAIL IN A PRINT
BY JOSEPH REDOUTÉ.

astonishingly popular? The answer lies in its ability to flower, not just in June and July, but all through late summer and into autumn, and with freedom too. Further Chinese imports found a receptive market, and for the first time in history the gardens of Europe now had crimson roses, miniature roses, glossy-leaved roses and climbing roses. These were soon being planted in parts of north America and newly colonised Australia.

In about 1809 yet another novelty arrived, a rose with pointed buds, silky looking petals and a spicy fragrance in its blush pink flowers. This became known as 'Humes Blush Tea-Scented', and together with its yellow form, it gave rise to the sweet and tender race of Tea Roses, prized for their elegance and beauty.

ROSES OF DELICATE PINK COMBINE WITH HONEYSUCKLE
IN A GARDEN OF OLD WORLD CHARM.

1812. It in turn gave rise to the Hybrid Perpetuals, whose big round flowers on stalwart bushes became hugely popular in the reign of Queen Victoria of England.

To marry the size and strength of the Hybrid Perpetual with the elegance of the tender Teas became the desire of Jean-Baptiste Guillot, nurseryman of Lyons. In 1867 he fulfilled his aim, and proudly showed 'La France' in the Paris Exhibition. He staged it at the appointed time, and waited for the judges' plaudits; he waited all that day, and the next, while his poor roses wilted in the heat; and when the judges did arrive, two days late, they gave him nothing. Fortunately, he was rewarded, for 'La France' soon became a prototype of the Hybrid Teas, the twentieth century's most popular garden roses.

The Guillot nursery also gave the world the first Polyantha rose, obtained from a climber that reached Lyons from either China or Japan. 'Ma Pâquerette' (which means 'My Daisy') bears clusters of small flowers on short free-blooming plants. White and pink forms soon ap-

Like the Teas, some Chinese roses fared badly in European winters, but fortunately they were able to interbreed with Old Garden Roses, producing offspring in which vigour, hardiness and a lengthily flowering period were combined. One such was the 'Portland Rose' from Italy. Other hybrids sprang up in unexpected places, such as South Carolina and Reunion in the Indian Ocean, and from them came the delightful Bourbons and Noisettes. These were repeat-flowering climbers, plants the like of which had never been seen in Europe's gardens, bearing blooms of exquisite petal form in a wide range of colours.

The French-sounding names reflect the contribution France made to roses at this time. The Empress Josephine's rose garden was created to hold every variety she could find. This not only made the rose a fashionable flower, but it also led to the appearance of new forms through natural interbreeding. One of these was 'Rose du Roi' with its rich red colour which was the sensation of

ROSES WITH THE LOOK OF A BYGONE ERA STAND PROUDLY
IN A MODERN BATHROOM.

THE BRILLIANT BLOOMS OF GLOWING ACHIEVEMENT ARE SET
AGAINST THE BUSH'S DARK FOLIAGE.

peared, and even a honey-yellow 'Perle d'Or' as a result of crossing with the Teas. The advent of a red small flowered rambler from Japan gave breeders the chance to extend the colour range. It was called 'Crimson Rambler' and was hailed as 'Rose of the Century'. It was introduced by 'Turner of Slough' in 1893 and Queen Victoria even journeyed to Slough to see it for herself.

THE STORY UP TO DATE

So rapid has been the evolution of the rose in the twentieth century that accounts of it fill many books. One such is *The Makers of Heavenly Roses* by Jack Harkness, which records the personal achievements of 17 major

CLIMBING OVER A CHARMING GAZEBO, PINK CLAIR MATIN IS
SELDOM WITHOUT FLOWERS DURING THE SEASON.

SYLVIA, WITH ITS DEEP PINK BUDS ON LONG, SLENDER STEMS, IS ONE OF REIMER KORDES' MOST STRIKING ROSES.

the first of what are now called Cluster-flowered or Floribunda Roses. It took years to achieve his dream rose, 'Poulsen's Yellow', but unfortunately its advent in 1938 was ill-timed. Others were quick to follow up his work, notably Kordes of Germany with 'Pinocchio', whose pink flowers have many petals like Hybrid Teas, yet are spaced neatly in the cluster. The American Gene Boerner then introduced the yellow 'Goldilocks', the salmon 'Fashion' and the amazing 'Masquerade'.

Everyone wanted roses in the aftermath of the War. From the world's leading breeders came many first-rate novelties. 'Queen Elizabeth' from Lammerts of California, a pink of amazing vigour; 'Iceberg' from Kordes, still the best white Floribunda, and 'Friesia' ('Korresia'), a sweet-scented yellow; from Tantau of Germany, a brilliant array of Hybrid Teas – 'Super Star', 'Fragrant Cloud', 'Blue

breeders. He tells how the work of Guillot was followed up in France by Pernet-Ducher, whose 'Soleil d'Or' of 1900 brought vivid flame and yellow genes into the Hybrid Teas, and Meilland, whose romantic family history is retold in Antonia Ridge's *For Love of a Rose*. François Meilland's prize variety 'Peace' (1942) bore yellow and pink blooms of flawless quality and great size on plants which set new standards for leafiness and vigour.

Svend Poulsen of Denmark crossed the free flowering Polyanthas with the Hybrid Teas and in 1924 launched the pink 'Else Poulsen', still popular in the USA, and

Moon' and 'Whisky Mac'; from Sam McGredy in New Zealand the exotic 'painted roses' – 'Picasso', 'Matangi', 'Sue Lawley' and many more. (Ralph Moore of California is famous in the rose world as 'Mr Miniature' for his single-minded application in improving the character of this group.) Ground cover roses are now becoming known, largely thanks to Onodera (Japan), Olesen (Denmark), Kordes and Noack (Germany) and Ilsink (Holland).

Britain's breeders scored with some notable Hybrid Teas, among them salmon pink 'Silver Jubilee' (Cocker 1978), apricot 'Just Joey' (Cant 1973), vermilion 'Alexander' (Harkness 1972) and yellow 'Freedom' (Dickson 1981). They and others have produced a range of Patio Roses and Floribundas. David Austin's new breeding lines provide old style blooms on repeat-flowering shrubs, and pioneer work on Climbing Miniatures by Chris Warner has already brought spectacular success.

THE PROFUSION OF SUBTLE SHADES OF PINK IS DISTINCTIVE OF THE BEAUTIFUL REGENSBERG.

With breeders resolved to keep trying for ultimate perfection, and with the existence of an ever-growing gene bank of better roses on which to work, the promise for the future of the rose is bright indeed.

LIGHT PINK CLAIR MATIN CASCADES OVER THE GARDEN WALL AND ITS WROUGHT IRON GATES.

TYPES OF ROSES

And I will make thee beds of roses
And a thousand fragrant posies

CHRISTOPHER MARLOWE (1564–93)

There are roses for everyone, for owners of both great estates and simple townhouse gardens. Roses are so varied that heights range from six inches up to fifty feet. They may be planted in containers on the patio, in beds, borders, even rock gardens. They may be used as ground covers or hedges, to clothe walls and fences, to run up pillars and old tree stumps, to romp over a pergola, or to grow as specimens in splendid isolation. Flower shapes may be cupped, pointed, rounded or rosette, and those with muddled centres are called quartered-rosette. They may have five petals or more than 50. There are all sorts of fragrances, and as far as colours are concerned, there is an enormous choice of reds, pinks, yellows, oranges, salmons, creams, whites, purples, lilacs, bicolours and blends, and there are even a few oddities in shades of brown and green. Out of the huge range of roses developed through the centuries, over 7,000 roses are commercially available today.

CLASSIFYING ROSES

Because roses are so versatile, efforts to classify them into distinct groups can never be considered final. For convenience, the following divisions are currently in use:

ITS CLEAR PINK PETALS AND MASS OF PURPLE STAMENS, MAKE DAINTY BESS ONE OF THE MOST LOVED SINGLE ROSES.

LA FRANCE, THE WORLD'S FIRST HYBRID TEA ROSE.

With the onset of winter, bush roses lose their leaves and become dormant. They need to be pruned before growth becomes advanced again in spring. Sharp secateurs are required, and the 'Felco' models are popular with keen rosarians, being light to hold with a good cutting action. A look at the plant will show which stems look young, green and healthy. These have the potential to carry next year's flowers. Prune away dead, diseased, ingrowing and feeble growths, then reduce the good stems and side shoots by up to two-thirds, or at the point where they approximate to pencil thickness. Exhibitors may cut the stems down further, leaving fewer outlets for the plant's sap. This results in a limited number of flowering stems with better quality blooms. Rose lovers whose dedication does not extend that far will get wonderful results, for roses are most obliging plants, ready to correct the pruner's faults. By observing how each variety grows, rose lovers will learn how to improve their pruning skills.

LARGE-FLOWERED BUSH ROSES (HYBRID TEAS)

Hybrid Teas are loved for the size and beauty of their flowers, their ability to bloom throughout summer and autumn, and their lasting qualities when cut. Some have an excellent fragrance, notably 'Fragrant Cloud', 'Rosemary Harkness', 'Deep Scarlet', 'Alec's Red', 'Double Delight' and 'Wendy Cussons'. 'Papa Meilland' has one of the sweetest scents of all, although it does not thrive in Britain.

Hybrid Teas grown to win cups at shows are called Exhibition Roses. In the USA 'Touch of Class', 'Keepsake', and 'Olympiad' head the list, while in the UK 'Admiral Rodney', 'Red Devil' and 'Grandpa Dickson' are keen favourites. Exhibition types may produce outstanding blooms but not in sufficient quantity to satisfy the general gardener.

A CORNER OF THIS BEAUTIFUL ROSE GARDEN IS EDGED WITH ICEBERG AND LAMB'S EAR.

CLUSTER-FLOWERED BUSH FLORIBUNDA ROSES

These bright, happy roses are well named, bearing, as they do, many blooms at the end of their sturdy stems. They are used a great deal in parks, where, as bedding plants, they give colour from summer to late autumn. In the garden they should be grouped in beds and borders for the best effect, or grown as a hedge. They are a great standby for cutting, especially for table arrangements and buttonholes.

The flowers vary from single to fully double according to variety, and growth habits differ too, the average height being 1 m (3 ft), though the stalwart pink 'Queen Elizabeth' may be as high as double or even treble that. For both garden and exhibition use, white 'Iceberg' and apricot 'Anne Harkness' are recommended by British experts, while 'Showbiz', 'Europeana' and 'Playgirl' head the charts in the USA. 'Trumpeter', which is rich scarlet and of a shorter growth, won the James Mason Medal in 1991,

TRUE TO TRADITION, FINE CHINA IS OFTEN EMBELLISHED WITH THE BEAUTY OF THE ROSE.

given to 'the rose that has given the most pleasure over the past fifteen years'. Fragrant Floribundas include yellow 'Korresia' and blush 'Margaret Merril'. The pruning method is as for Hybrid Teas.

DAVID AUSTIN'S CONSTANCE SPRY HAS ALL THE CHARM OF OLD ROSES.

PATIO OR DWARF CLUSTER-FLOWERED ROSES

These are like small-scale versions of the Floribundas. The word 'patio' calls to mind an area for garden relaxation, where narrow borders, spaces in paving,

THE REEVE HAS TALL, ARCHING STEMS AND DEEPLY CUPPED PETALS.

CLIMBERS AND RAMBLERS

Ramblers are of rather untidy growth, with several stems rising from ground level, and although there are a few exceptions, they bear clusters of small flowers in spectacular profusion just once a year. Among the most familiar are 'Albertine', American Pillar' and 'Dorothy Perkins'. Others well worth growing are 'Blush Rambler', 'Goldfinch' and 'Crimson Shower'.

Ramblers will cascade down a bank, grow against a trellis, cover a small fence, and decorate pergolas and arches.

Most Climbers have bigger flowers, and include varieties of bush roses. 'Climbing Ena Harkness' and the

ornamental tubs and troughs give opportunities for small plants to flourish. These delightful roses are well-adapted to bringing colour and brightness even to the smallest garden. Top favourites in the UK include the sweetly named light pink 'Gentle Touch', orange red 'Anna Ford' and apricot 'Sweet Dream'. The same principles of pruning apply for other bush roses, and although the stems are thinner, they need to be pruned hard to maintain a neat, cushiony growth habit.

THE BRIGHT BLOOMS OF PAUL'S SCARLET TUMBLE ELEGANTLY OVER OLD STONE PILLARS.

FRAGRANT WINNER'S CHOICE, WITH THEIR FULL AND HIGH
CENTRES, ARE IDEAL EXHIBITION ROSES.

between 5-20 cm (2-8 in) long, depending on the thickness of the stems. Climbers vigorous enough to grow up trees can be left alone, apart from the removal of dead wood. One such is 'Rambling Rector', described by Graham Thomas as 'impenetrable, unprunable, overpowering'.

When it comes to choosing an item for a pergola or fence, to grow against a wall or around a pillar, there really is nothing more charming than a climbing rose.

STANDARD OR TREE ROSES

Standards are sometimes called High Stem roses. This gives an indication of their purpose, which is to provide colour at eye level. They are lovely for adding impact to a mixed border, where they lend height and elegance, standing proud among their neighbours.

'Clg Iceberg' are two well known examples. 'Clg Cecile Brunner', which bears petite pink flowers, is a more productive source of blooms than its spindly bush form. Climbers on dry sites need to be well watered during drought periods in spring and early summer.

When pruning, take out old or weak stems, tie the strong young main stems either horizontally or slantwise (or in the case of a pillar, spirally), and trim back side shoots that have borne flowers so that they are left

CREPESCULE, AN OLD NOISETTE ROSE, IS USUALLY
SEEN AS A RAMBLER, BUT HERE AN UNUSUAL STANDARD HAS
BEEN CREATED.

Nurserymen propagate the varieties grown as Standards near the top of upright stems, so that the shoots grow out to form bushes at an elevated level. Weeping Standards are the result of budding ramblers on to the stems; when the trailing shoots emerge, they bow towards the ground under the weight of foliage creating a living umbrella effect.

Stem heights vary according to the type of rose – taller for Weepers, and 1 m (3 ft) or less for Miniatures. Miniature Standards are perfect for containers, borders or beds, where they can be surrounded by miniature roses or other low-growing plants.

MINIATURE ROSES

These are the smallest growers of all, and they derive from 'Rouletii', a rose of mysterious origin cultivated in pots in Switzerland, and described as only 5 cm (2 in) tall by its discoverer, with rose red petite full-petalled blooms. Most miniatures reach 30-46 cm (12-18 in), though the height depends on how they have been grown; plants budded on an understock will grow bigger

THE MINIATURE FLOWERS OF A POTTED SWEET CHARIOT ADD A TOUCH OF ELEGANCE TO THE GARDEN.

than those raised by cuttings or tissue culture. The tiny replica miniature blooms reflect just as wide a variety of flower forms as exists in other types of rose.

Miniatures may be used as edging plants and are ideal as pot plants. They create colourful cushions in the rock garden, and those with a trailing habit are perfect to plant in hanging baskets, so that they overflow with blooms. Children have a special affection for these small roses, a few of which placed in an egg cup can make an instant arrangement. Miniatures promote keen rivalry between exhibitors, and at the UK's First National Miniature Show in 1991, the winning roses were brought over from California packed in ice! The pretty orange blends 'Little Jackie' and 'Arizona Sunset' stole the honours on that day.

Miniatures need the same attention at pruning time as other dwarf bush roses. Those of a trailing habit, like 'Red Cascade' and blush 'Nozomi', should only be cut back if they are exceeding the available space.

SHRUB ROSES

These include some of the loveliest roses of all. Most grow larger and leafier than bushes, and they have an amazing variation in growth and character, for they include wild (species) roses, Old Garden (Heritage) Roses, and newer types such as Ground Cover roses. They grow easily, and though some require considerable space, no rose garden is complete without a few shrub roses.

Some wild roses are suitable for the garden. Among these are *R. glauca* or 'Rubrifolia', famous for its reddish leaves, *R. stellata mirifica* which has flowers of deep rose purple and strawberry-like leaves, and the bright single yellow 'Canary Bird'. The *R. rugosa* group make wonderful rounded plants with flowers in white, pink or purple. These do well even in indifferent soil.

BETTY PRIOR AND FORGET-ME-NOTS CREATE A SYMPHONY OF PINK AND BLUE IN A BUSY GARDEN.

The Old Garden Roses include Albas, Gallicas, Centifolias, Damasks, and their descendants. Of these, among the strangest and most beautiful are the Mosses, which have a moss like covering over the stems and buds. The charm of these old roses is endearing, and their survival is ensured by the formation of Heritage Rose Societies in the USA, Britain and elsewhere. The roses' strong points are their beauty, fragrance, vigour, and the freedom with which they cover themselves in bloom; the drawbacks are their limited range of colour (for they are mostly pink and white) and their inability, with only one or two exceptions, to flower more than once a year.

THE UNUSUAL CREAMY BEIGE OF ANTIQUE SILK CAUSED A SENSATION WHEN THE ROSES FIRST APPEARED.

THE INTRIGUING HISTORY OF THE WHITE ROSE OF YORK
IS SURPASSED ONLY BY ITS MAJESTY.

Roses from the Orient introduced new colours and extended flowering times, and their influence is shown in shrub roses of more recent years. Notable are Pemberton's Hybrid Musks, graceful shrubs with handsome leaves and dainty sprays of bloom; his shell pink 'Penelope' (1924) still wins prize cards at the shows. Pemberton's gardener, Bentall, followed up with 'Ballerina', whose massed hydrangea heads of apple-blossom blooms are an annual delight. 'Graham Thomas', from England's David Austin, successfully combines the quartered shape of old roses with features they did not have – a bold yellow colour, and remontancy of bloom. In Germany, Wilhelm Kordes worked with 'Max Graf', an American rose of creeping growth, and from that line many ground covering roses are now being introduced, improving year by year in quality of bloom.

The premier award in the Royal National Rose Society's prestigious trials has been won by ground cover roses in three of the last five years. The winners are 'Mary Hayley Bell' (deep pink), 'Kent' (white) and 'Little Bo-Peep' (blush).

The correct pruning of shrub roses depends very much on the variety. Many Old Garden Roses flower on the previous year's wood, and so the long young shoots they carry should not be pruned more than half their length. Bigger shrubs and wild roses require simply the removal of dead or diseased wood, and the clearing out of ingrowing or cross-rubbing stems.

CULTIVATING ROSES

*There is no rose bush whatsoever
but prospereth the better for
cutting, pruning, yea and burning*

PLINY (C. 61–113)

Few shrubs reward the gardener so richly as a rose. What do roses need to give their best?

The first essential is fertile soil. Roses do well in different soils, as long as they are not *very* acid or *very* alkaline, and as long as the ground is well-drained. If normal garden plants are thriving, the soil should suit roses well.

They will not be happy in boggy ground, so avoid wet places. Nor is it wise to put a new plant in the place of an old one without exchanging the soil with soil from a site where roses have not been growing, or using a soil steriliser such as Bradosol.

Light is the second essential need. Roses do best where the sun will shine on them at least a few hours in the day, and they must be away from the shade of trees and substantial shrubs. If they are deprived of light, the plants grow spindly, as though reaching up or out to catch their sunshine ration.

EXQUISITE PINK ROSES ARE PERFECTLY COMPLEMENTED BY
THE LACY WHITE OF SNOW-IN-SUMMER.

RAMBLING DOROTHY PERKINS, BLUSHED WITH HEALTHY PINK, ENFOLDS A BRONZED GARDEN STATUE.

Roses are plants of the open air, but there are limits to what even these generally robust plants can stand. Incessant cold draughts or powerful winds will inhibit their growth. In constantly windswept gardens the best answer is to provide a hedge or erect a small fence for shelter.

PROPAGATION

CUTTINGS

The simplest method of propagating roses is by cuttings, but not all roses strike readily. Pinks and reds seem easier than yellows and flames, and ramblers and Old Garden

*Man could have lived his life till
    evening's close
Humbly and worthily without a Rose.
But One who knew his weakness
    and his might
Made Roses, not for need,
    but for delight*

FAY INCHFAWN,
NRS ROSE ANNUAL 1928

Roses are the easiest of all. Many new roses are protected by patents or breeders' rights, and home gardeners can propagate them for personal enjoyment, but not for sale.

To take cuttings, select pieces of half-ripened wood in late summer, cut them into lengths of about 15 cm (6 in) (less for miniatures) and trim them to just below an eye at the base, and just above one at the top. Trim off the lower leaves and insert them into pots filled with equal measures of peat, moss and soil, or John Innes No. 2 compost.

Three could go into one 18cm (7 in) pot, and rooting hormone can be used. Keep them damp but not too wet, and do not keep them in full sun; a cold greenhouse, conservatory or sheltered location out-of-doors all make a good environment.

Cuttings that survive will form their own root system. This may take up to eighteen months, though miniatures root more quickly. When they seem to be ready, transplant them into individual pots in winter or spring, and harden them off for use in the open garden.

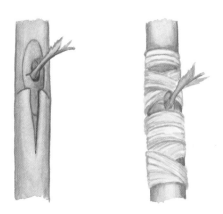

a sharp knife to slide the eye away from its stem with a sliver of wood behind it. Make a T-shaped cut close to the base of the stock, peel the bark carefully back and slip the eye in. Bind with a budding tie to keep the eye in place. Nearly all commercial growers propagate by this method. The rule about protecting roses applies as in 'Cuttings' above.

BUDDING

This involves increasing stock of a variety by using budding eyes (the growing tips in the junction between leaf and stalk and stem). The objective is to insert the eye into the basal wood of another plant specially grown to receive it, usually a form of *R. laxa* or *R. multiflora*. Use

THE SUBDUED HUES OF THE ROSE MINGLES WELL WITH PASTEL SHADES OF LAVENDER.

MASQUERADE AND DONALD PRIOR CONTRAST WELL WITH THE FOXGLOVES AGAINST A BACKDROP OF COPPER BEECH.

DREADED PESTS

Select healthy varieties and give them constant and loving attention, and they will grow with vigour and give good blooms, and their good health will help enormously in combatting any pests and diseases which may attack them. But like all plants in the garden, there are times when roses cannot survive on love and care alone, and may be affected by a variety of pests.

Greenfly can build up from small numbers to a multitude with amazing speed, so check young shoots and squash any greenfly individuals you may find. In a garden full of roses, concentrate on plants in the most sheltered places which greenfly seem to prefer. If spraying is a necessity, ICI Rapid Greenfly Killer (active ingredient pirimicarb) is recommended by the UK *Gardening from Which?* magazine as one that spares the friendly insects — bees, ladybirds and lacewings.

POT LAYERING

This method works well in warmer climates. Bend a pliable stem into a U-shape, place the base of the U into a small plastic pot and tie it into place by threading string through the holes in the bottom of the pot. Fill the pot with compost and keep it damp. This will encourage a root system to develop, after which the new plant can be severed from its host.

SEED

Rose seeds are found inside the hips that ripen in late autumn. They may be harvested then, chilled to help break down the hard seed casing, and sown in seed compost before the onset of spring. Keep the compost moist, not waterlogged, and in a temperature not above 60 °F. Seedlings that germinate should be grown on until they appear strong enough to transfer into seedling compost. Germination is not easy, so there can be no guarantees.

MINIATURES, BUSHES AND CLIMBERS THRIVE UNDER THE EAVES OF A QUAINT THATCHED ROOF.

A PROFUSION OF PINK ROSES ADDS A TOUCH OF WARMTH TO
A SETTING OF OLD WORLD CHARM.

THE SICK ROSE

O Rose, thou art sick!
The invisible worm
The flies in the night,
In the howling storm.

Has found out thy bed
Of crimson joy,
and his dark secret love
Does thy life destroy.

WILLIAM BLAKE

Red spider mites become a serious nuisance in hot weather, spinning fine webs under the leaves which appear dried out and dusty. Roses close to masonry are likely to be the first affected. The mites are difficult to control, but they very much dislike cold water directed in a strong jet on their hiding-places. An early watch for distressed leaves and a prompt follow-up with the water treatment may well prevent a major problem. Bio Long-Last (sold in Australia as Rigor☆ active ingredients dimethoate/permethrin) is recommended.

Of fungus troubles, rust is the most insidious. It often starts underneath the lowest leaves, which take on a yellowish look. If on inspection they carry tiny orange or black globules, action must be taken. Remove affected leaves, and give the nearby roses a preventive spray. The best specific is pbi Systhane (active ingredient myclobutanil). Plants readily susceptible to rust should either be destroyed or planted well away from other roses.

WOBURN ABBEY, SIMPLE ANNUALS AND BRILLIANT
BOUGAINVILLEA CREATE A PICTURE OF VIBRANT COLOUR.

Blackspot is unsightly, but late attacks cause little harm. An early summer attack is serious, so watch for the signs, and use a recommended spray like pbi Dithane 945 (active ingredient mancozeb) if necessary. Varieties known to be susceptible should be sprayed preventively.

THE SOFT PINK OF ROSA RUGOSA IS CONTRASTED AGAINST ITS DEEPLY VEINED LEAVES.

TAKE CARE WHEN SPRAYING

Insecticides can be highly dangerous indeed, and extreme care should be taken in their storage and their use. Do not mix them in cold drink bottles, which could tempt small children into drinking them. If you have young children, be sure to keep the sometimes lethal concoctions out of the reach of curious, little hands.

Most pests and diseases are controllable and, if a close watch is kept on your garden, especially in the early weeks of growth, any potential problems can be more easily overcome. If pests are dealt with quickly and efficiently, they should pose no serious threat to the splendour of the garden.

Mildew targets plants which are at a disadvantage, such as those in dry sites, or in persistent draughts, or in places where air cannot freely circulate. Once started, it can spread with great rapidity. Care should be taken not to have roses in obviously vulnerable places, and to avoid planting highly susceptible varieties. If an attack begins, water the affected plants freely and try ICI Benlate (benomyl) or Nimrod-T (bupirimate, triforine), a triforine-based rose spray. Late autumn attacks can be ignored, as they do no lasting harm.

A ROSE CALENDAR

My love is like a red, red rose
That's newly sprung in June.

ROBERT BURNS (1759-1796)

This calendar follows the seasons, beginning in winter, the most dormant period of the year. Winter in the northern hemisphere corresponds to December, January and February, and in the Antipodes to June, July and August. Because we live in a world of differing climates, the calendar notes should be taken as a general guide, adaptable to local circumstances – for there will be plants wholly dormant under winter frost and snow in Montreal and Norway, at the same time as roses in Bermuda and Portugal are eager to grow in conditions of sunshine and refreshing rain. It is always a good idea to seek advice from nearby nurseries or horticultural groups about treatment of roses in your own locality, so that you can be aware of your plants' needs as they progress through the year. Only you will know the particular conditions of your rose garden, so make notes on how they look, how they grow and how they bloom, so that you can build up lessons for the future. Share your knowledge by joining a national or local rose society.

THE ANCIENT CHARM OF A STONE BIRD BATH IS
HIGHLIGHTED BY A PROFUSION OF SOFT PINK BLOOMS.

THE BEST-SELLING ICEBERG IS OFTEN SEEN AS A STANDARD AND MIXES WELL IN A BORDER.

THE WINTER SEASON

Will the roses survive? That is the anxious question asked in cooler climates, when the only visible evidence of roses in the garden is a series of snow hummocks and pillows beneath which they lie.

The answer is almost certainly yes, because rose plants are tough, and snow in fact plays a protective role, warding off dehydrating winds and the effects of alternating spells of frost and sunshine. But survival does depend on planting the right varieties, and on giving protective treatment where needed. There are some shrub roses bred especially for their hardiness, such as 'Pike's Peak', raised by Griffith Buck in Iowa and 'William Baffin' from Felicitas Svejda of Ottowa. These should withstand prolonged spells of frost. Others, such as the elegant Teas, are not frost hardy, and are therefore unlikely to survive hard winters unless special care is taken. For the greater majority of roses no winter protection is required. If it is likely that temperatures will fall below −20°F for any length of time, as in parts of the USA, Canada and northern Europe, then some covering is advisable. A useful practice is to cover up the plants with whatever protective material is available, e.g. straw, peat, moss, buckwheat hulls, soil, bark chippings, or even newspapers stapled together to form a collar. Modern materials such as microfoam and Poly-e-foam (expanded polythene) mounted on a frame have been found effective as a covering for whole beds and to protect climbers. Standard (or tree) roses are vulnerable because the head is so exposed. One method of safeguarding them is to bend them over so that they lie upon the ground − a rather drastic expedient since some roots may have to be cut to achieve this. For climbers, burlap can be wrapped round the stems to protect them from the effects of freezing winds. The timing of winter protection is important − it must not be applied too soon. This is where local advice can help you.

As has been said, most rose lovers do not need to take these steps, although a mulch (or covering) between the plants will help reduce the degree to which the soil becomes frostbound, thus encouraging earthworms to be more active and maintain fertility.

When the soil is free of frost during the winter months, it is a good time to plant new roses from the nursery. They will be supplied with the roots bare of soil at this season, having recently been harvested from the nursery

THE MAGNIFICENT COLOUR OF PAUL'S SCARLET MAKES IT A FAVOURITE FOR COVERING ARCHES AND WALLS.

RED AND WHITE ROSES

Read in these roses the sad
  story
Of my hard fate and your
  own glory:
In the white you may discover
The paleness of the fainting lover:
In the red, the flames still feeding
On my heart with fresh wounds
  bleeding,
The white will tell you
  how I languish,
And the red express my anguish:
The white my innocence displaying,
The red my martyrdom betraying,
The frowns that on your
  brow resided,
Have those roses thus divided:
Oh! let your smiles but clear
  the weather,
And then they both shall
  grow together.

THOMAS CAREW

fields. Sometimes a parcel sent by mail will arrive during a period of frost. If this happens, the best advice is to leave the parcel unopened, keep it in a cool place, such as a frost free garage or shed and then plant the roses out as soon as the ground is fit. If the parcel has been opened, dip the plants in water for a few minutes to refresh them, them wrap polythene round them to avoid dehydration. If there is likely to be a long interval (more than three weeks) between receipt and planting, the roses should be heeled in. This is done by digging a shallow trench in frost free ground, and covering the roots and lower parts of the stems with fine soil, peat or a similar material. That way the plants will be safe for several weeks.

The conditions that best suit roses – an open site in well drained soil – have already been described. Roses need to be planted firmly and at the correct depth. A hole 16-20 cm deep (6-8 in) is usually large enough to accommodate the roots, but it does depend on the rootstock that is used, so check the plant before you dig the hole. Most bare-root roses have their roots system at an angle to the stems. If you lean the plant back against the straight edge of your hole, the roots can be spread out to take their natural direction. Overlong rootlets can be trimmed off with sharp secateurs. It is sensible to dip the roots before planting so that they are wet when they go into the ground – but there is no advantage in soaking them for long periods. Cover the roots of the plant with an equal mix of fine soil and moistened peat or coir compost together with 60 g (2 oz) of sterilized bonemeal. When the hole is nearly full, tread the material down so that it is meshed closely round the roots, then fill up the hole, tread firmly again, and finally hoe over the surface so that the soil is level. If you can see the stems clean of soil to the point where they spring from the rootstock, you have them at the correct depth; the depth is important because the roots like to feed at the correct level.

If standard (tree) roses are being planted, set a stake at planting time and secure it to the plant just below the head and just above soil level; a third tie halfway between can be made on taller stems.

ICEBERG, ALSO AVAILABLE AS A SHRUB OR STANDARD, GRACES THE WHITE, WOODEN BEAMS OF A PATIO.

Winter is a good time to clean tools, overhaul secateurs and pruning saws, plan for new plantings and check your fertilisers and sprays. If you have roses in pots, now is the time to transfer them to larger containers. For those that are to stay in the same container, renew the top 7-10 cm (3-4 in) of soil, replacing it with compost such as John Innes No. 3 to which a sprinkling of rose fertiliser has been added. Keep the compost damp but do not over-water, and make sure the pots drain adequately. Roses in the glasshouse can be allowed a temperature of 40-45°F but remember that extra heat without sufficient light will encourage the growth of non-flowering stems.

THE SPRING SEASON

Spring is the time for planting, pruning and feeding. The method of planting bare-root roses has already been described. Those that were put in during autumn and winter should be checked in case frost action has loosened them. Give the stems a light tug, and if there is any movement, tread the plant in firmly. As warmer weather comes, the plant should start to sprout. If any young plant is slow in this respect, the best first-aid treatment is to give it a bucketful of water, and when the soil is dry, to tread round it to tighten the roots in the soil.

The method of pruning established roses has been described under 'Types of Roses'. For those that have been newly planted, the best treatment if they are HT's, Floribundas, Dwarfs or Miniatures is to cut the stems so low that they are left like two or three fingers sticking out

PINK ROSES, WITH THEIR SOFT, MUTED SHADES, TRAIL GENTLY OVER A GARDEN WALL.

of the soil. It is usually safe to leave the stems of new shrub roses about 15-24 cm (6-9 in) long, of new climbers 38-60 cm (15-24 in) long, and of new standard (tree) roses about 15 cm (6 in) long from the point at which shoots grow from the budding union at the top of the standard's stem.

The time for pruning will vary according to climate. It should be carried out when the plants are coming out of dormancy and before growth is too advanced. After pruning your roses, make sure that all the cut stems have been cleared away.

It is at this point that the soil should be hoed, to aerate the surface and prevent early weeds from sprouting and running rampant – but watch out for companion plants and bulbs. Take particular care to hoe or chip over any depressions caused by footprints, which may spread out and form impermeable crusts on heavy soils if not broken up.

After pruning time, the soil is more accessible than at any other season, and this gives you an excellent opportunity to apply a mulch. Mulching has been called the natural method of soil formation, because it is essentially a ground-covering litter of fallen leaves and other organic matter. Its object is both to provide food as the young plants begin to grow and flourish, and to help conserve the moisture in the ground.

Roses need food and they need moisture even more, because their roots can only feed on dissolved material. Therefore it is best to apply mulch when the ground is wet, after a good rain or watering. All sorts of materials are used for mulching, depending on what is available; leaf-mould, coir compost, old grass cuttings, hop manure, rice hulls, sludge – all these are homes for bacteria and will create beautiful flowers for your enjoyment. Apply a

layer of mulch which is up to 10 cm (4 in) thick if you can afford it, but keep it a few centimetres clear of the bases of the plants. Remember that the roots are feeding under the soil between the plants.

Towards the end of the spring period, rose food can be added and hoed into the surface of the soil or the mulch. There are many brands on sale, all containing the three main food elements, nitrogen (N), phosphorous (P) and potash (K), plus lesser amounts of others such as magnesium, calcium and iron, all of which are essential for healthy growth. Used as directed; often this will mean an application in spring and further ones at three weekly intervals through the summer months. Remember that in order to take in the food, the plants need moisture, so water them during dry spells. Be especially sensitive to the needs of climbers in dry wall sites; giving them a bucketful of water once a week can make all the difference between a languid performance and a brilliant show.

Spring should be blessedly free of pests, but on warm days your local over-wintering aphids will emerge. Keep an eye out for them and rub them off gently when you spot them; it will forestall having to cope with thousands later. This is particularly important for roses in the greenhouse, which is a paradise for early aphids.

TRUE TO ITS NAME, THE BLOOMS OF CAREFREE BEAUTY ARE SCATTERED HAPHAZARDLY OVER THE BUSH.

THE SUMMER SEASON

The stage is now set for a summer of beauty, and it is a time for observing the progress of the plants carefully. Insect pests such as aphids and caterpillars must be expected. If you have a small number of roses and inspect them frequently, these pests can be rubbed or picked off. Otherwise you can spray your plants, preferably with a substance which spares the friendly insects such as ladybirds and lacewing flies, as mentioned previously in 'Cultivating Roses'. If you see leaves twisted into a tight tube, you may be sure that these will have been visited by the leaf-rolling sawfly, which will have laid its eggs in some leaves. Remove and burn the leaves to prevent the eggs from hatching out.

Continue watering and hoeing to encourage steady growth and keep down weeds which may have sprung up; hoe slowly, so as not to disturb the feeding rootlets. Further mulching and feeding can be provided. If suckers appear, remove them from the point of origin. When it is a few centimetres high, a sharp tug will often dislodge a

FLOURISHING EVEN IN CONTAINERS, THERE ARE FEW PLACES IN THE GARDEN WHERE ROSES WILL NOT THRIVE.

sucker growing from the rootstock, saving the need to dig down to it. If you are not certain whether a shoot from near the base is, in fact, a sucker or not, leave it to grow until you can be absolutely sure; sooner or later a comparison of leaves and thorns with those of the cultivated rose will help you make the right decision. Do not think that just because you have discovered seven leaflets you have found a sucker.

When flower buds appear, disbudding will ensure top quality blooms if you wish to exhibit them at shows. Keen exhibitors use cones to protect the choicest HT blooms. Show schedules need careful study to ensure entry deadline dates are met and the rules are well understood. When the plants are growing fast it is a good time to buy a foliar feed from the garden centre to spray on the leaves; it must convey some benefit, though how beneficial they are is debatable.

As summer advances, look out for further pests such as those described in our 'Cultivating Roses' section, especially red spider mites and rust which, because they appear underneath the leaves, can easily go unnoticed. Tired-looking climbers on walls are likely targets for red spiders, and also for leafhoppers, small green insects which bob up and down on the surface of the upper leaves. Some, but not all, aphid sprays are effective against leafhoppers too. Beetles that chew the leaves and petals of garden flowers are a problem in some countries; pyrethrum-based insecticides can be used to combat these pests.

There are certain rules to observe when spraying. Use an efficient sprayer, mix the spray very carefully according to the instructions, never spray in hot sunshine – the early morning or cool of the evening is the best time; clean the sprayer after use and keep the chemicals well away from children.

When the roses have flowered, dead-head the varieties that you know will flower again. It is important to do this as soon as the petals fade and drop, because otherwise the plant will quickly direct food into the hip where seed is forming, thus delaying the production of new flowering shoots. Remember not cut off more stem than you need to when dead-heading – cutting back to the nearest promising set of leaflets will be sufficient. Ramblers that do not flower again should have some of the older flowering shoots removed, so that new growth has enough space to grow and ripen. Keep watering, feeding and hoeing so that all your plants continue to grow healthily. Some growers prune away weak basal growth on their bushes at this time, to remove vulnerable targets for rust and blackspot.

During summer, shows are held, gardens are open and nursery fields astonish visitors with their acreages of colour. It is a wonderful time to visit, look and learn – and select new roses for the garden. You can plant roses in containers, provided you have prepared the ground. Use the same planting mixture as for bare-root roses, but try to keep the soil block round the potted rose intact when planting, so that the roots can feed and grow without any interruption. Tread the plants in well and keep them watered until they are established.

THE AUTUMN SEASON

Many roses continue to bloom during the autumn but it is not wise to feed them late, because this stimulates end-of-season growth that will not ripen; just enjoy the flowers as a gardener's bonus. Sulphate of potash at the rate of 60 g (2 oz) per plant can be applied in early autumn, as a means of hardening the wood against the colder months.

In late summer or early autumn the ground should be prepared for new rose plantings. There is no single recipe for preparation, because it varies according to the state of the soil. The important point is that it must be carried out in time for the ground to be settled and firm when the planting is to be done. On average soil, allow three to four weeks between preparation and planting. On very heavy soil, more time may be needed for cloddish lumps to break down.

THE ENDEARING PINK BLOOM OF MARY ROSE.

A WIDE RANGE OF COLOURS IS REFLECTED IN THIS BASKET OF ROSES PICKED IN THE FULL FLUSH OF AUTUMN.

When working the ground, remember that the human foot is one of the soil's worst enemies, especially when the ground is wet. If you must tread on the bed, chip your footmarks over with a hoe or a small spade.

During the later weeks of autumn it is useful to tidy up the plants for winter. Climbing roses can indeed be pruned at this time, and their newly grown long shoots can be trained in place, ready to provide next summer's blooms. Other roses can be trimmed by cutting back their overlong stems so that they will be neater in appearance, and less liable to be rocked by winter's gales. Ties on standard stakes – and the condition of the stakes themselves – should be checked, to make sure that the plants will stand fast. Preparation should be made for winter protection in areas which require it.

Thus the cycle of the year is completed. The roses will have given the greatest enjoyment to those who have pursued their hobby with enthusiasm, following the precepts of the calendar; even neglectful gardeners among us will have been rewarded well beyond our desserts.

If the soil is well-drained, deep digging is not essential; but if rainwater lies on or near the surface, then drainage must be provided. In normal garden soil this means digging down to the lower soil and breaking it up. In special circumstances, such as where the work is too physically demanding, or in a place where the water table is naturally high, it is possible to make a raised bed so that the roots will be in drier ground. The lower soil will also need breaking up if on inspection it proves to be compacted, so that earthworms and other subterranean creatures cannot thrive; such garden soil is effectively 'dead'.

Digging a new bed provides a marvellous opportunity to add all kinds of bulky feeding material to the soil, such as compost, manure and bark – anything which will enrich the fertility of the ground. If the lower soil is being turned over, take care that it remains in the lower level and that the topsoil goes back on the surface.

ROSES

Nature responds so beautifully
Roses are only once-wild roses,
*   that were given an extra chance,*
So they bloomed and filled themselves
*   with coloured fullness*
Out of sheer desire to be splendid,
*   and more splendid.*

D. H. LAWRENCE (1885-1930)

LEARNING MORE ABOUT ROSES

For evenings and dark winter days, books are a valuable resource. They can help you if you are uncertain what to plant, or need practical advice, or want to learn in greater depth about the lore and history of the rose. Many books are a pleasure to handle, thanks to superb colourwork. A few are so well written as to be considered literary classics. Out of hundreds to choose from, here are a few suggestions among more recent works:

The Rose Expert (pbi Publications 1988) by Dr D G Hessayon. Inexpensive, comprehensive and concise.
Roses (Dent 1978) and *The Makers of Heavenly Roses* (Souvenir Press 1985) by Jack Harkness. The first concerns the genus, and the second the breeders.
The Complete Book of Roses (Timber Press 1981) by Gerd Krüssman. Weighty, useful for reference.
Rose Growing Complete (Faber 1976) by E B LeGrice. Well written, covers all aspects of rose growing and breeding.
The Old Shrub Roses (Dent 1978), *Shrub Roses of Today* (Dent 1974) and *Climbing Roses Old & New* (Dent 1979) by Graham Stuart Thomas. Scholarly and stylish.

HONEY SUCKLE AND CLAIR MATIN OBSCURE A THATCHED CHALET, WHILE ALBERTINE CREATES A DRAMATIC BACKGROUND TAPESTRY.

A Heritage of Roses (Unwin Hyman 1988) by Hazel Le Rougetel. Fascinating research into rose history.
Roses at the Cape of Good Hope (Breestraat-Publikasies 1988) by Gwen Fagan. Informative; splendid pictures.
Roses (Harvill 1991) by Peter Beales. Encyclopaedic, describes 1900 varieties, many illustrated.
Old Roses and English Roses (Antique Collectors' Club 1992) by David Austin. Good style and pictures.
The Ross Guide to Rose Growing (Lothian 1991) by Deane Ross. A wealth of information from Australia.
The Book of Classic Old Roses (Mermaid 1988) and *The Best of Modern Roses* (Pacific 1987) by Trevor Griffiths. Zestful writing by New Zealand grower, many photographs.
Roses of America (Henry Holt 1990) by Stephen Scanniello. Good on roses in the USA.
Living with Roses (Ludwig's, POB 28165, 0132 Sunnyside, Pretoria) by Ludwig Taschner. Thorough and practical.
The Photographic Encyclopaedia of Roses (CLB 1991) by Peter Harkness, co-author of this book. History, cultivation, descriptions, many illustrations.

COMPANIONS FOR ROSES

The lily is all in white, like a saint,
*   and so is a mate for me:*
And the daisy's cheek is tipped with
*   a blush*
He is of such low degree:
Jasmine is sweet, and has many loves,
And the broom's betrothed to the bee:
But I will plight withe dainty rose,
For fairest of all is she.

THOMAS HOOD (1799–1845)

Although roses look spectacular in large beds in public parks and wonderful in private gardens, they can be accompanied by other plants whose colour will enhance that of the roses or bring a permanent green to the garden. In fact, parsley planted near to a rose bush, will even serve to improve the magnificent fragrance of its blooms.

Hedges and other plants growing behind the roses play an important part in the overall effect. The dark burgundy of berberis, for example, will complement clear pink or crimson roses beautifully, and golden conifers are the perfect foil for yellow roses. Thus, it is important to take the background plants into account.

FRENSHAM OF BRILLIANT SCARLET CONTRAST HAPPILY WITH PINK ROSES AND MAUVE OXALIS.

ALYSSUM SPREADS A SCENIC WHITE CARPET ALONG THE
GARDEN PATH LINED WITH ICEBERG ROSES.

When you plant companion plants for your roses, remember that the roses should dominate the bed or border. They must be in full sun and not be over-shadowed by other plants. Additional plants must be regarded only as complementary and those which are found to be too vigorous, thus depriving roses of sun and nutrients, should be removed immediately.

The only time at which the soil around the roses can be cultivated is at pruning time when the plants are dormant. Digging at any other time may damage the roots near the surface. It is therefore logical that any plants which are to act as companions to the roses must not be planted too close to the main stem, as this will necessitate disturbing the soil and the mulch. The only exception may be small seedlings, and the seed of annuals such as alyssum and myosotis, which may be sewn directly into the soil around the roses. But even these should not be planted too close as they could interfere with the weekly soaking so necessary for your roses.

If your beds contain roses of many colours, you will need to take some care when choosing companion plants. It is best to play safe with grey-leafed plants such as lamb's ear, and almost any blue flowers you can think of, as blue is a most obliging colour and will seldom clash with others. Other suitable plants for the multi-coloured rose garden are the white flowers – alyssum, white irises, violas, stocks, liliums and many, many others.

ANNUALS

Many annuals live quite happily with roses, either in their midst or on the edge of beds and borders. Good edgers include alyssum, bedding begonias, violas, petunias and dianthus. To lend height, either among the roses or at the back of the bed, you could plant foxgloves, pentstemons, delphiniums and even verbascums. Verbascum, however, is a striking yellow and care should be taken in the choice of its neighbours.

One advantage of annuals is that many of them can be obtained in separate colours, making it possible to work out colour schemes.

GROUND COVERS

Ground covers can serve a dual purpose. They look pretty and keep the soil surface cool, but they do need to be kept in check as they could come too close to the rose stems, and so cut off their supply of food and water. Ajuga and Lamium are among the more suitable ground covers and, in colder areas, the low-growing veronica, with its blue flowers, is truly lovely. Also ideal for cold gardens is *Cerastium tomentosum*, also known as Snow-in-Summer, which forms a carpet of grey leaves creating a perfect foil for pink or red roses. Lamb's ear has leaves of a soft grey, and can be used as an edger or as a ground cover.

MRS SAM McGREDY MIXES QUITE HAPPILY WITH A VARIETY OF OTHER GARDEN PLANTS.

A CURVED BORDER SHOWS OFF THE REFINED ELEGANCE OF PLAYBOY, MICHELLE MEILLAND AND ICEBERG ROSES.

LAVENDER

Lavender and rose go together in a charmingly old-fashioned way. Lavender spilling over onto a path and backed by bush roses or standards is a heart-warming sight and where roses have been allowed to grow untrammelled, there is no better companion than one of the many scented 'geraniums', particularly one of the rose- or lemon-scented varieties.

PERENNIALS

Those perennials which complement roses are liliums and irises. If it can be kept in check, the Japanese or wind anemone is a suitable adjunct to the autumn rose. And for those spaces between there are no better companions for climbing roses than members of the clematis family. There are many plants which will complement and grow well with roses, and they should be selected according to their height, shape and colour. Also never forget the grey-leafed plants which will show up the magnificent colour of your roses.

HERBS

In days gone by, roses were planted together with herbs and, because they were once regarded as herbs themselves, there is now a natural affinity between them. Experiment by planting borage, with its hairy, grey leaves and vivid blue flowers, or feverfew which has pretty white flowers. Rosemary is a herb which beautifully complements roses, but it is rather too vigorous for planting in the middle of a rose bed. It is better to plant it to one side or, if there is a wall behind the bed, to allow it to cascade prettily off the edge of the wall. Its attractive flowers and delicious scent are an added bonus.

FIREFALLS OF GLOWING RED REACH OVER TO GREET A SINGLE, BEARDED IRIS.

A VISION

A rose, as fair as ever saw the north,
Grew in a little garden all alone:
A sweeter flower did nature ne'er
*   put forth,*
Nor fairer garden yet was
*   never known:*
The maidens danc'd about it
*   morn and noon,*
And learned bards of it their
*   ditties made:*
The nimble fairies by the
*   pale-fac'd moon*
Water'd the root and kissed
*   her pretty shade.*
But well-a-day, the gard'ner
*   careless grew:*
The maids and fairies both
*   were kept away,*
And in a drought the
*   caterpillars threw*
Themselves upon the bud
*   and every spray.*
God shield the stock! If heaven
*   send no supplies,*
The fairest blossom of the
*   garden dies.*

WILLIAM BROWNE

45

A SPECTACLE OF COLOUR

*I sometimes think that never
blows so red
The Rose as where some buried
Caeser bled.*

OMAR KHAYYAM (1050–1123)

There is such a vast range of rose colours that it is quite possible to cause clashes, not only between different colours, but between the different shades and tones of a particular colour. In the pinks, for instance, some have a blue tinge, while others have a salmon tinge, and the two shades simply do not complement each other.

There are also varying shades of red, orange and coral. Yellows can be both pale and deep, and there are subtle shades of white and bicolour, as well as those elusive beiges and buffs.

The safest way of blending is to bring the rose flowers together, but height must also be considered. You could have a background of climbers or ramblers, with standards and bush roses in front, and then miniatures and ground cover roses at ground level. These may all be of the same colour, or subtle blends, or even contrasts, and it is well worth the effort to take care and time over the choice of colour.

A HAPPY PROFUSION OF ROSES IN A CRYSTAL BOWL BRINGS
A LITTLE OF THE OUTDOORS INTO THE HOME.

FRIESIA PERFORMS EXCEPTIONALLY WELL AND PRODUCES
A SUCCESSION OF CLUSTERS OF MAGNIFICENT BLOOMS.

A combination of gleaming white Icebergs and lilac-pink
Escapades, or other pink and even yellow roses, is soft
and gentle on the eye, whereas the same Iceberg combined with Trumpeter is rather startling.

If you prefer roses of a single colour, you can plan an
unbroken cascade. Chooses tall shrub roses or standards
for the rear of the bed, and lower bushes for the middle
which will, in turn, give way to miniature standards with

Although many gardeners believe that colours in nature
simply cannot clash, there are also those who feel that
bright and vibrant hues assembled together may detract
from the individual beauty of each plant. It is for this reason that many people favour plants with grey or subdued
foliage to intersperse with the gay colours of their roses.

A sea of roses in the same colour may be rather dull,
while a patchwork of colour may look quite garish. It
may be a good idea to find a comfortable compromise
between the two extremes. Red roses may pose a particular problem as there is such a wide variety that the different shades may well clash. It may therefore be better to
separate them with white, cream or even yellow varieties.

There is a vast selection of colours from which to
choose and, although some gardeners like to have a happy jostling of colours, there is no doubt that a bed containing roses of one or two shades is extremely pleasing.

AS WITNESSED BY THE SPLENDOUR OF DALLAS, NATURE'S
PALETTE HAS PAINTED MANY ROSES WITH VIVID COLOUR.

THE PURE WHITE OF SNOW-IN-SUMMER HIGHLIGHTS THE GENTLE PINK OF THE ROSES.

Once you have decided on a one-colour garden, you may like to add an edging of plants of another colour. Low-growing, pale blue myosotis, also quite commonly known as forget-me-nots, will create delicate pools or cushions of colour among pink or white roses.

The combinations of colour, however, remain a matter of personal taste and your garden is, after all, there largely for your own pleasure.

miniature roses, and ground covers at their feet. This can be an absorbing task, and a demanding one, for there are many shades of red, pink and yellow. Pinks may be salmon or bluish; reds may vary between orange and near-black; and yellows may be pale or apricot, and combinations of the more extreme shades may not always be as striking as you had imagined.

Roses, their sharp spines being done,
Not royal in their smells alone,
But in their hue:
Maiden pinks, of odour faint,
Daisies smell-less, yet most quaint,
And sweet thyme true.
WILLIAM SHAKESPEARE (1564-1616)

THE SILVERY UNDERSIDE OF THE PETALS OF LADYLIKE ARE A PERFECT COMPLEMENT TO ITS GLOSSY, DARK FOLIAGE.

THE RAINBOW'S END

Roses are renowned for their glowing colours – the pristine white of 'Virgo', 'Pascali' and 'Polar Star'; a multitude of pinks from the delicate 'Margaret Merril', with its slightly ruffled petals, to the deeper pink of 'Anna Livia', chosen by the City of Dublin to mark its millennium and a premier award-winning Floribunda. And, being the most romantic of colours, pink roses have been given equally romantic names – 'Bride's Dream', 'First Love', 'Lovely Lady' and 'Gentle Touch'.

Then there are the reds in many shades and tints. 'City of Belfast' has touches of orange showing through, 'National Trust' is a clear red, and 'Charles Mallerin' and 'Papa Meilland' are of the deepest possible red.

The search for a truly red rose was a long one. 'Etiole de Hollande' caused a stir, but this was a mere ripple compared with the storm of applause given to 'Crimson Glory' when it appeared in 1935 – and not only was this rose a deep, velvety red but it was also heavily scented. Then followed 'Ena Harkness', 'Mme Louis Laperriäre', 'Oklahoma' and many others of the deepest red.

ORANGE SENSATION, WITH ITS STARTLING MASS OF DEEP, ORANGE BLOOMS, LIVES UP TO ITS NAME.

Clear yellow roses are not as plentiful as other colours, and the creation of a good yellow was the dream of many breeders. Working with 'Persian Yellow', a yellow shrub rose, France's Pernet-Ducher made some crosses in 1883. After ten years he found a marketable seedling, and in 1910 'Rayon d'Or' came out, the first pure yellow Hybrid Tea. His best rose was 'Souvenir de Claudius Pernet', one of the most popular yellows. The name evokes a bitter memory, for Claudius was one of Pernet-Ducher's sons, both of whom perished in the First World War.

ALTHOUGH YELLOW ROSES ARE SAID TO SIGNIFY INFIDELITY,
THEIR GOLDEN BLOOMS ARE BREATHTAKING INDEED.

Today Pernet-Ducher's rose lives on in the genes of many fine roses whose shades vary from gold to palest yellow. Now we have a fine selection from which to choose – 'Courvoisier', 'Buccaneer' and the fragrant 'Korresia', also known as 'Friesia'.

The colour of some roses can be difficult to describe. Can one, in all fairness, call 'Buff Beauty' a creamy beige? And what of the so aptly named 'Antique Silk'? Its perfectly formed blooms are reminiscent of old lace and have the sheen of satin. Now this beige has been taken a step further with the introduction of the enchanting 'Julia's Rose', the darling of the flower arrangers.

A green rose? There is *Rosa chinensis viridiflora*, whose freakish spiky flowers give it curiosity value if little else. But there is also 'Greensleeves', whose petals start life a creamy pink before gradually turning a delicate, but definite, green. 'Limelight' also has a touch of green, but this time it is distinctly lime in colour.

VIBRANT PINK ROSES MINGLE FREELY WITH CAMPANULAS,
PENTSTEMONS AND FOXGLOVES.

BECAUSE OF ITS EXCEPTIONAL COLOUR, ANTIQUE SILK HAS BECOME A FAVOURITE OF BRIDES.

'Blue Moon' and 'Shocking Blue' are close and both have a hint of blue in their mauve petals, as do 'Blue Nile', 'Blue Danube', 'Charles de Gaulle' and 'Harry Edland', but a rose of true sky blue is still the stuff dreams are made of. In 1991 Australian scientists announced that they had isolated the gene responsible for blue colour in flowers, and they were planning to introduce it into roses. Their next task will be to find a rose flower – probably of creamy-yellow colouring – which will accept a Petunia gene. This is far from easy due to the complex chemistry involved. The team are hoping to complete the first stages by 1994 and to have a rose by the year 2000. It may take years, but one day no doubt the world will admire and acclaim the First Blue Rose.

There are also the bi-colours, some of them in surprising combinations. The crimson and cream 'Double Delight' has long stems and can produce perfect blooms, making it ideal for the vase. Then there is the mauve-tipped red of 'Paradise' (also called 'Burning Sky'), and the pink stripes of 'Candy Stripe'. Some roses, like 'Masquerade' and 'Judy Garland', change colour with age, pinky-red replacing yellow to give an unusual multi-coloured effect.

Despite this glorious diversity of colour among roses, there is still a deep and burning ambition among rose breeders to create the first truly blue rose. They used to say that watering the roots with indigo would create blue blooms, but the closest breeders came were with 'Violette', a rambler with small purplish flowers fading to mauve, a rose still cherished but certainly not blue, and a delightful Polyantha bush, little more than ankle high, called 'Baby Faurax'.

CREATING A NEW ROSE

I have heard the mavis singing
His love song to the moon;
I have seen the dewdrop clinging
To the rose just newly born.

CHARLES JEFFRIES (1848–87)

Unbounded patience, devoted care and immense skill lie behind the introduction of a new rose, which can take ten years at a cost few breeders choose to calculate, but which must run to several thousand pounds. And out of every 20,000 seedlings raised, perhaps only one will have the potential to become a new and splendid addition to the catalogues. Happily there are those who have an enduring and persistent ambition to create the perfect rose, who are prepared to wait and watch, to choose carefully from the new young plants.

The choice of parents is all-important and once the choice is made, the breeder embarks on the long journey from pollination to ultimate selection.

On a sunny day in early summer, when the first buds are about to open on the selected mother plants, some are selected for pollination. The petals are removed and the pollen-bearing anthers cut away so that the flowers cannot pollinate themselves. Pollen from a different variety which has been programmed to act as the 'father' is brushed on to the mother flower's receptive stigma, and a tube extruded from the successful grain of pollen then conveys the father's genes to combine with the mother's in the ovaries, to form a seed which inherits both parental

THROUGH METICULOUS PRUNING AND ATTENTION, A PEACE CLIMBER HAS PRODUCED A HARVEST OF BEAUTIFUL BLOOMS.

genes in a unique combination. They say the same two roses could produce 250 million different offspring had anyone the patience and resources to put it to the test.

As the seeds ripen the familiar rose hip begins to form. The father's name is inscribed on a label around the stem, so that if any of the seeds fulfil the breeder's dreams, the vital birth certificate is not lost. When the hips are ripe in autumn, they are harvested and their contents carefully stored, away from mice. Before being sown, the seeds are treated in an effort to break down the hard casing that surrounds them. A thorough chilling is one method, and others are secrets closely guarded by the breeders, because it is not the *obtaining* of the seed, but its *germination* that is the hardest task.

After sowing, the first miraculous signs of growth appear in very early spring; two seed leaves break the surface of the soil, looking most un-roselike. As they grow, true rose leaves appear, and imagine the excitement when

MRS JOHN LAING IS A HYBRID PERPETUAL WHICH PRODUCES LARGE FLOWERS OF SOFT PINK.

THESE PALE, OLD ROSES GROW FREELY AMONG OLD STONE PITCHERS ON A RUSTIC VERANDAH.

A FLORAL TEA SERVICE OF FINE CHINA LENDS AN AURA OF DAYS GONE BY TO AN ELEGANT TABLE SETTING.

after a month or two the first flower buds open, each one the only specimen of its kind in the whole wide world, destined perhaps to be, like 'Peace', the prototype of countless million clones – or more likely, destined for oblivion and never to be seen again, except perhaps in your memory.

Each and every seedling is examined and evaluated. Those which show no signs of promise are mercilessly weeded out, and heartrending decisions have to be made concerning the borderline varieties which have only a very limited potential.

The reject pile contains plants whose blooms have shown scorch marks from the sun, or which have suffered from malformation, weak growth, or poor colour, or those which are too similar to others on the market or susceptibility to mildew. Those that pass the test do so on

A GARDEN FEATURE OF A STONE LION IS SURROUNDED BY ROSE GERANIUM AND DAINTY BESS.

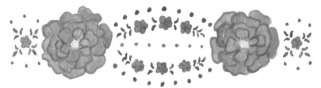

VALERIANS, FORGET-ME-NOTS AND PELARGONIUMS TUMBLE DOWN A BANK ACCOMPANIED BY OLD ROSES.

LeGrice, Pearce and Warner in England; Croix, Delbard and Meilland in France; Kordes, Tantau and Noack in Germany; Onodera in Japan; McGredy in New Zealand; Dickson in Northern Ireland; Cocker in Scotland; and Carruth, Christensen and Moore in the USA.

Also in the USA, Robert Basye of Texas is promoting research work to improve the breeding potential of the world's wild roses. Use of the techniques of modern science will aid the creation of disease-resistant forms, and promise, in his words, 'to unlock the treasures of the entire rose genus'.

grounds of vigour, fragrance, health, unfading colour and pretty form. These promising seedlings are then budded on to healthy stock, viewed for another season, and the cream survive for rebudding and further years of trial.

After three or four years, a final decision will be made concerning the commercial value of the remaining seedlings. Some will be sent to testing stations round the world in Europe, Japan, New Zealand and the USA. Results from these trials within the next three years will help the breeder in his final choice of which varieties to offer to rose growers. They will usually be offered under licence, whereby the breeder receives a royalty for each plant the grower propagates or sells.

This, very briefly, is the story of the creation of a new rose. Meticulous work is involved and breeders grow many thousands of seedlings each year in the hope that something truly spectacular will arise out of their diligent and patient labours. The professionals who are most active in this task today are Menäve in Belgium; Olesen in Denmark; Austin, Barrett, Cant, Fryer, Gandy, Harkness,

GROWING HEALTHY ROSES

I always loved to call my lady Rose,
For in her cheeks do roses sweetly glose:
And from her lips she such sweet
*   odours threw,*
As roses do 'gainst Phoebus'
*   morning view.*
But when I thought to pull't, hope was
*   bereft me,*
My Rose was gone, and nought but
*   prickles left me.*

HENRY LICHFIELD (FL. C. 1613)

What are the secrets of growing healthy roses? Good cultivation, correct siting and an eagle eye for signs of trouble are important. A basic rule is to obtain healthy plant material in the first place. Most plants sold are budded, which means the lower part is the root system of a wild understock, and the stems on top belong to the named rose. A budded rose can be thought of as 'two half-roses'. *Both halves* need to be healthy when they enter your garden.

THE PERFECTLY SHAPED BLOOMS OF DREAM DOLLY ARE
SALMON PINK WITH A DEEPER SHADE IN THE CENTRE.

What can go wrong with the rootstock? A virus may cause strange patterns on the foliage, and will spread through the plant, leading to wilting or loss of vigour and eventual ruination. Also, aphids can pass the virus from one plant to another. Rootstocks grown from *cuttings* are the most virus-prone. Check that if cuttings have been used, the stocks have been certified virus-free. Roses budded on seedling briars, i.e. grown from *seed*, should be all right, as the virus is not transmitted via the seed. In Britain, seedling briars are almost always used.

The cultivated stems are normally healthy, but they can harbour fungus spores. The stems are routinely checked by government inspectors when plants are destined for export, both during active growth, and before despatch. Many countries have stringent rules and insist that imported roses be grown for some months in quarantine. If you buy plants from an exporting nursery, that is a good guarantee that they will be healthy because the necessary inspection standards will have been met.

FREE-FLOWERING PENELOPE IS A HYBRID MUSK WITH A DISTINCTIVE MUSK FRAGRANCE.

Choosing the right varieties is also an important factor. Look around you, see what thrives best in your locality. Visit a rose trial, or study the results published by rose societies. Roses on trial will have been scrutinised by judges looking for the least sign of trouble, and the winners should be good prospects. In Britain a Disease Resistance Trial has just become established; the best performer to date is a ground cover rose called 'Flower Carpet', with HT 'Alexander' and Floribunda 'Princess Michael of Kent' also performing well.

Fungi (and insects) may be a plague one year, and virtually absent for the next three. For gardeners, one fact is certain: if you buy healthy plants from a reliable source and give them a modicum of care, they will be better able to resist any enemy that comes.

BECAUSE OF ITS UNUSUAL CREAMY COFFEE AND HINT OF MAUVE, JULIA'S ROSE IS AN ETERNAL FAVOURITE.

concentrate the flow of sap into just a few favoured blooms. Floribundas may need similar disbudding, and the removal of the centre flower.

Most shows cater for other types of rose as well, and recently the 'Three Stage' class has become popular, in which budding, opening and fully expanded blooms of the same variety are arranged together. A delightful new way of showing Miniatures has been devised, involving the use of artists' palettes.

Many prefer to cut their roses in the early morning, when the stems are likely to have more water in them. If it is not possible to do this, wait until the cool of the evening. Place the stems in lukewarm water as they are cut, and then transfer them to a container filled with lukewarm water. Chrysal or Floralite in the water will greatly

A lovely being scarcely form'd
or moulded,
A rose with all its sweetest leaves
yet folded

LORD BYRON (1788–1824)

THE SHOW

One of the most rewarding experiences for many gardeners is to walk away from a flower show secure in the knowledge that, after maybe years of tending and caring for a garden, all that effort has been recognised and acknowledged with an award.

Bringing blooms to ultimate perfection does not happen without dedication and weeks of planning. To show a Hybrid Tea involves pruning it more than normal. This is done in winter or early spring, and the precise timing of the operation is all part of the overall skill involved and differs according to the variety of rose. When growth appears, side flower buds are removed at a very early stage. The object of both these operations is the same: to

TAUSENDSCHON BRINGS A LIGHT TOUCH TO THE CAST IRON PILLARS, AND FRAMES THE ROSES BEYOND.

order to make the rose look as natural as possible. Camel hair brushes – even human breath – can be used to encourage a backward flower to part its petals. Do not forget the foliage; by moistening it with a damp cloth to remove splash marks – or greenfly – you may tip the balance in your favour in an even contest.

By trial and error the 'right' treatment will be found. As one exhibitor has written, 'The best way to learn is to do it.' If you do not win, congratulate the winner, and work out why the judges decided as they did. Next time you will be more experienced, and therefore have a better chance. Perhaps next year the 'Star' or 'Queen' of the show will carry your name on the prize card.

extend the flower life. When transferring the flowers, remove the bottom leaves and the lower thorns, to avoid overcrowding and to provide more access points for moisture. The ideal place to store the flowers will now be to put them in a dark cool place, which has good air circulation but not draughty, for several hours. If refrigeration is used, note for future reference how well or badly the different varieties respond.

Re-check the schedule of the show to make sure you know the venue and the judging time and do not have to rush. When showing several HTs together, let the finest bloom occupy pride of place, to draw the eye towards it, and grade the rest so that larger blooms are towards the back and smaller ones towards the front. If there is a variety of colours make sure that they either harmonise or balance each other. If wool ties or pellets have been used, remember to remove them. Petals can be manipulated in

THE BRILLIANT WHITE OF ICEBERG IS COMPLEMENTED BY THE SUBTLE HUES OF TRAVESTI.

A PERFUMED GARDEN

*Yet the rose has one powerful virtue
  to boast,
Above all the flowers of the field:
When its leaves are all dead, and fine
  colours are lost,
Still how sweet a perfume it will yield!*

ISAAC WATTS (1674-1748)

What is perfume? The word, quite naturally of French origin, means 'by way of smoke' and goes back to the early days when the first perfumes arose from boiling pots and the fires of aromatic wood intended to counteract the stench of charred flesh. And from those early barbaric origins, we have today the very essence of civilisation and sophistication.

There is surely nothing as evocative as a scent. Just a whiff will bring back memories of childhood, or the recollection of both sad and happy times. As Kipling so aptly put it: 'Scents are surer than sights and sounds to make your heart strings crack.'

Perfumes have always been associated with seduction and allurement. One of the most vivid images of Cleopatra portrays her aboard her heavily scented barge, which is covered with a thick carpet of roses to impress Mark Antony. And Roman women were never without their perfumed oils, sachets of rose petals, and 'rhodium', a perfume made from rose extracts. Roman men were equally fond of their scents, but Julius Caesar made his opinion quite clear when he told a highly perfumed dandy, 'I would rather you stank of garlic.'

ARCHES OF ICEBERG ARE THE PERFECT FOIL FOR THE PINK
ROSES IN THIS NATURALLY FRAGRANT GARDEN.

THE WONDROUS FRAGRANCES OF ROSES HAVE BEEN CAPTURED IN PERFUMES FOR CENTURIES.

When buying roses, ask about the perfume, or smell them yourself if you want a heavily scented garden. Many modern varieties are fragrant, notably 'Alec's Red', 'Compassion', 'Double Delight', 'Fragrant Cloud', 'Gertrude Jekyll', 'Jacqueline du Pré', 'Margaret Merril', 'Papa Meilland', 'Paul Shirville' (called 'Heart Throb' in New Zealand), 'Rosemary Harkness' and 'Sheila's Perfume'.

Damask roses are grown in Bulgaria, India, Saudi Arabia and elsewhere to produce attar of roses, the prized essence which is worth more than its weight in gold. The roses are picked soon after sunrise, when the petals contain the maximum amount of fragrant oils. After distillation, three grades are produced for market. Alba roses may also be used; their yield does not compare with that of the Damasks, but by being planted on the margins of the rosefields they can provide some protection for the rest of the field.

A different process at Grasse in the south of France makes use of Centifolia roses, which provide attar and rose wax, both in demand by the cosmetics industry.

Queen Elizabeth I of England had her own recipe for a scent made of musk and rose, and the floors of her palaces and castles were liberally sprinkled with rosewater.

Rose perfumes are many and varied, but all have the distinct fragrance of the rose. And how difficult they are to describe! Fresh, clean, heady, strong, sweet, heavy, light. Some have spicy scents, and some even smell of apples. And it is somewhat disheartening to think that those scents were not created for our delight alone, but to attract moths, butterflies and other insects for pollination.

There is a strange story that roses 'lost' their scent. The truth is that 'Persian Yellow' and some Chinese roses, which as we have seen introduced new colours and repeat-flowering ability to western gardens, were lacking fragrance. Yet such was the demand that 'Parson's Pink China' and the early Chinese reds, despite their want of scent, were very popular. We cannot blame gardeners for desiring such wonders of the age. Nor was any scent 'lost' since the old standbys were then – and are now – still available. Only nature is to blame.

MYTHS AND LEGENDS

Then, in some strange eventful hour,
the earth produced an infant flower.
The gods beheld this brilliant birth
and hailed the rose, the boon of earth.

ANACREON

The rose is mentioned in many myths, legends and fairy stories passed down from one generation to the next. The sleeping princess was surrounded by a thorny hedge of roses before she was awakened by her charming prince, and Beauty's father went in search of the perfect rose to save his daughter from the clutches of the Beast. There is also the tale of the dear old woman who had two lovely daughters, each as beautiful as the red and white rosebushes at either side of her cottage door, and so she called them Snow White and Rose Red. And then there was little Thumbelina whose bed quilt was a single, fragrant rose petal.

FELICIA COVERS THE ARCH WHILE IMPROVED CECILE BRUNNER NESTLES AGAINST THE WALL.

A SEDATE LADY IN AN ORNATE BRASS FRAME IS SURROUNDED BY LOOSELY ARRANGED ROSES.

And what of Alice in Wonderland? She came upon three gardeners applying red paint to white roses, and when she asked the reason, they explained that they had mistakenly planted a white rose tree where the Queen had wanted a red one, and that she would surely have them beheaded if she found out.

THE FLOWER OF THE GODS

Like many flowers, the rose often played an important part in the ancient religions of both the East and the West, and was particularly prominent in Greek and Roman mythology.

Zephyrus, the West Wind, had failed to win the favours of Flora, the Roman goddess of flowers, and the only way he could attract her attention was to transform himself into a flower which Flora would find utterly irresistible. This he did, and Flora was won. And the irresistible flower was the rose.

*If Zeus chose us a king of the
 flowers in his mirth,
He would call to the rose, and
 would royally crown it:
For the rose ho!, the rose is the grace
 of the earth.
Is the light of the plants that are
 growing upon it:
For the rose ho! the rose is the eye of
 the flowers.
Is the blush of the meadows that feel
 themselves fair.
Is the lightning of beauty that strikes
 through the bowers
On pale lovers who ist in the glow
 unaware.
Ho, the rose breathes of love! ho, the
 rose lifts the cup
To the red lips of Cypris invoked for
 a guest!
Ho, the rose having curled its sweet
 leaves for the world
Takes delight in the motion its petals
 keep up.
As they laugh to the wind as it
 laughs from the west!*
SAPPHO (C. 612–580 BC)

HERITAGE OF PALEST PINK GENTLY SUGGESTS SERENE
TRANQUILLITY OF YESTERYEAR.

this old variety with its neat habit and sweet fragrance makes a delightful garden rose and is as popular as the renowned poet himself.

In Persia, as in Greece and Rome, roses were linked with ideas of beauty, love and wine. Legend has it that the lotus had been Queen of Flowers but, as it slept by night, Allah graciously enthroned the white rose in its stead. This delighted a nightingale which, enraptured by the beauty of the flower, snuggled up close and began to sing its praises. Caught up in its song, it did not feel the thorn

Today, the rose is still associated with true love and is the flower of St Valentine, patron saint of sweethearts. The flower was also consecrated to Venus, goddess of love and courtship, as an emblem of beauty, and to Cupid as a symbol of love. According to myth, Cupid gave a rose to Harpocrates, the god of silence, to bribe him not to betray the many amours of Venus. As a result, the flower also became the symbol of silence, and was sculpted on the ceilings of banquet rooms and over confessionals. Today, the term *sub rosa*, meaning 'under the rose', still signifies secrecy.

Omar Khayyam, the famous Persian mathematician and astronomer who lived *c* 1050-1123, was so moved by the natural world that he turned to poetry and became known to the west as the author of the *Rubaiyat*.

Khayyam often wrote of roses, and a pretty pink Persian rose was planted on his grave in Nishapur. Seed was collected there in 1884 and over 100 years later, a cutting planted in 1893 on the grave of Edward Fitzgerald, translator of Khayyam's quatrains. Named 'Omar Khayyam',

which pierced its breast and stained the petals crimson – in this way introducing red roses into Persia. The theme of the nightingale and the rose became a favourite with poets and painters, both in Persia and beyond…

A ROSE OF HISTORY

Fifteenth-century England's savage civil strife is famous in history as The Wars of the Roses. Yet none of those who fought in it ever used that title. In fact, it wasn't invented

The rainbow comes and goes,
And lovely is the rose.
WILLIAM WORDSWORTH (1771-1855)

STARTLING RED ROSES ARE A STRIKING CONTRAST TO THE PURE WHITE OF LILIUM LONGIFLORUM.

THE BEAUTY OF A GARDEN ENHANCED BY ROSES IS SURPASSED ONLY BY ITS RAINBOW OF COLOURS.

until 1829 when Sir Walter Scott who is renowned for his historical novels used the term. The conflict arose because there were two rival claimants to the throne. The badge of Lancaster was a red rose, that of York a white one. Shakespeare's *Henry VI* implies that the contenders made their choices from a bush bearing different coloured roses in London's Temple Garden. In fact links between roses and the English crown extend even further.

It all started with Eleanor of Provence, who became Queen of England in 1236, and adopted as her badge a golden rose. Badges were a mark of identity, useful for baggage, retainers' livery and in processions. Eleanor's golden rose was adopted by her elder son. The younger

son, Edmund Earl of Lancaster, changed the rose's colour to red, a convention which was to be passed down to his descendants through the years. A white rose badge belonged to the Earls of March, whose heiress married into the family of the Duke of York. The existing Yorkist badge was a dull rose of 'blue and mulberry' hue, and the white rose from the Earls of March now replaced this as being more prominent and distinctive.

After thirty years of war, Henry Tudor married Elizabeth of York, thus uniting the red rose and the white and bringing to a close the strife. In this strange way, the Tudor rose came to be the emblem both of the royal house, and of the nation and the nation's peace.

When shall the stars be blown
about the sky,
Like the sparks blown out of a
smith die?
Surely thine hour has come, thy
great wind blows,
Faroff, most secret, and
inviolate rose?
ROBERT HERRICK (1591–1674)

PITCHERS FILLED WITH ROSES ARE A FITTING COMPLEMENT TO FINE, OLD CHINA.

FOLKLORE

Man blessed with both creativity and imagination and, inspired by the awesome beauty of the Queen of Flowers, has enriched both his culture and his language with a splendid array of imagery and symbolism. And the rose plays not a small part in this heritage.

We have already discovered that the red rose is seen as a symbol of many, many facets of humanity: love, war, blood and faith. But roses, in their infinite variety of colour and shape, have come to mean so much more. The white rose stands for purity, rosebuds for youthful beauty, and single roses for simplicity. The Burgundy Rose also implies simplicity and beauty; the China Rose, grace and everfresh beauty; the Daily Rose, a smile; the Dog Rose, that beauty is your sole attraction; the Moss Rose, voluptuous love; the Provence Rose, my heart is in flames; the Musk Rose, whimsical beauty; the white rosebud, too young to love; the white rose, full of buds, secrecy; a wreath of roses, beauty and virtue rewarded; the yellow rose, infidelity; a faded rose, fleeting beauty.

Even the calamity of bubonic plague which raged through Europe in the seventeenth century brought with it the connotation of the rose:

TUSSIE-MUSSIES OF ROSES, HERBS AND OTHER FLOWERS WERE SUPPOSED TO WARD OFF DEATH AND SICKNESS.

A WEEPING STANDARD OF SEA FOAM PRODUCES SHOWERS OF SMALL WHITE BLOOMS.

Ring a ring o'roses
The dreaded rash of the plague

A pocket full of posies
herbs to keep the plague away

A-tishoo! A-tishoo!
the fatal sneezing

We all fall down
dead, of course

THE NAME OF THE ROSE

What's in a name? that which we
call a rose
By any other name would smell
as sweet.

WILLIAM SHAKESPEARE (1564–1616)

Shakespeare's point of view is not always shared by nurserymen, who are aware how easily an unfortunate name can deter customers. Between say 'Benson & Hedges Special' and 'Fragrant Cloud' or 'Comtesse Icy Hardegg' and 'Lovely Lady', there is little doubt which are more fitting names for a rose.

The first rose list is found in the works of the elder Pliny, who died in AD 79 in the eruption that destroyed Pompeii. Eight of the eleven names on his list bear the names of places – the rose of Campania, of Miletus and so on; the others have names indicating their character, one very spiny, one very full of petals and one useful for a garland. Naming roses because of where they came from or what they looked like continued well into the eighteenth century. Naming them after people was very rare. Indeed the first such rose is thought to have been 'Singleton's Hundred-leaved', named after a gardener who died in 1735.

This all changed when the rose became a fashionable flower in France, as the following story reveals. A fine crimson rose, the sensation of 1812, was raised in the gardens of the palace at St Cloud, and promptly named by the administrator Comte Lelieur for himself as 'Rose

A SQUARED TRELLIS PROVIDES A CAPTIVATING BACKDROP FOR QUEEN ELIZABETH AND ICEBERG.

The longest rose name is reputed to be 'Souvenir des Fiancailles de l'Archiduc Rodolphe d'Autriche et de la Princesse Stephanie des Pays-Bas' in 1880. And the shortest name, which is for, as you would expect, a miniature rose, is 'Si'.

Bad rose names, like good ones, are a matter of taste and judgement. Who would plant 'Atombombe', which the raiser renamed 'Atomflash' before giving it a third and

Lelieur'. Louis XVIII, seeing it on return from exile, expressed a wish to have it renamed 'Rose du Roi'. The ink on the labels was hardly dry when Napoleon escaped from Elba, causing it to be changed to 'Rose de l'Empereur' – until Waterloo, when it reverted, this time for good, to 'Rose du Roi'.

So began the fashion for naming roses for top people which has continued ever since. New roses still bear royal names, the most recent being 'Princess Royal', 'Duchess of York', 'Princess Alice' and 'Empress Michiko'. Personalities of stage and screen are favoured such as 'Judy Garland', 'Bob Hope', 'James Mason' and 'Nigel Hawthorne'. Political namings carry risks; sales of 'Neville Chamberlain' plummeted in 1939, and who wants to be remembered for raising 'Adolf Hitler'? Far safer to serve fashion, arts and sport, with the likes of 'Gary Player', 'Picasso', 'Handel', 'William Shakespeare', 'Christian Dior' and 'Jacqueline du Pré', or towns and cities, with 'Chicago Peace', 'City of Auckland' and 'Southampton'.

THE GENTLE COLOURS OF CASANOVA MAKE THIS SPLENDID ROSE A UNIVERSAL FAVOURITE.

SURELY THE MOST FAMOUS OF ALL THE ROSES, PEACE HAS
A PERMANENT LOOK OF SERENE BEAUTY.

PEACE

The Meillands, whose name is synonymous with roses, had produced many outstanding varieties in the south of France. Then the Second World War broke out and communications collapsed. Fortunately, there had just been time to send the budwood of a promising new seedling, Number 3.35.40, to Germany and Italy. And, in the last package to leave the American Embassy, there was a small parcel of budwood addressed to Mr Robert Pyle, a rose grower in America and a friend of the Meillands.

So the plants were propagated for trial in countries separated by the conflict of war. As the young shoots grew, all who saw them were delighted at their vigorous growth, handsome foliage and good health. The appearance of the blooms, yellow with pretty hints of pink, lived up to these first impressions and surely exceeded everyone's expectations – save those of the breeders who must have known they had a winner.

final cloak of decency as 'Velvet Robe'? 'Angel Dust' sounds delightful until you find it has another meaning as a narcotic drug. Perhaps the best names of all are those that evoke the character of the flower, especially its colour or its fragrance. 'Double Delight', 'Pink Parfait', 'Golden Showers', 'Fragrant Dream' – these are examples of fine and expressive names.

But often the stories behind the roses are as interesting as the names themselves.

NOT ONLY BREATHTAKINGLY BEAUTIFUL, PEACE IS ALSO GENEROUS IN ITS BLOOMING.

The breeders named the new rose 'Mme Antoine Meilland' in memory of Papa Meilland's wife and offered it in France in 1942. In Germany it was sold as 'Gloria Dei', meaning 'Glory of God' and in Italy as 'Gioia' or 'Joy'.

Its introduction in America was eagerly awaited by rosarians, who bestowed on it one of their highest honours, the Portland Gold Medal, in 1944. Not until 29 April 1945, the day on which Berlin fell, was number 3.35.40's destiny made known. 'Peace' was presented at a special ceremony with the words: 'We are persuaded that the greatest new rose of our time should be named for the world's greatest desire: Peace. Towards that end, we dedicate this lovely new rose to Peace.'

And when the peace conference was held in the United States in California, one Peace rose was placed by the bedside of each delegate.

And so Peace, a rose of exquisite beauty and a sweet perfume, made its delicate, noiseless explosion upon a world crying out for something lovely, and since the first day of its naming, hundreds of millions of plants have been sold, and have filled the hearts of their new owners with pride and joy.

*He who would have beautiful roses
in his garden
must have beautiful roses in his heart*
S. REYNOLDS HOLE,
DEAN OF ROCHESTER

CRIMSON GLORY

Rose growers had long searched for a good red rose, and when Kordes of Germany presented this bloom of a rich deep red, with closely packed petals, good form and a heavy perfume, it was applauded far and wide.

Is it not strange to think that this rose, renowned for its fragrance, had as its parents two scentless roses, 'WE Chaplin' and 'Catherine Kordes'?

But while these roses were the immediate parents of Crimson Glory, its ancestry included many wonderfully scented roses.

MME CAROLINE TESTOUT

Mme Testout was a Parisian couturier with only moderate success and fame, until she had the foresight to pay for the privilege of having a rose named after her in 1890.

The rose chosen was not regarded as anything special by the grower but, once named, it become a bestseller, won a gold medal and is still available. And Mme Testout herself prospered greatly.

PENELOPE AND BLUE GERANIUM CREATE AN ENGLISH COUNTRY LOOK IN THE GARDEN.

AMERICAN BEAUTY

This rose began life in France in 1875 as 'Mme Ferdinand Jamin', crimson-carmine in colour, full of petals and with a delightful fragrance. It was not a great performer in the garden, but under glass it gave perfect blooms.

Like many roses of that era it would soon have been forgotten had an entrepreneur not taken it to the USA and changed the name. 'American Beauty' had irresistible appeal, and carried the rose on a wave of affection well beyond its normal life expectancy. In 1925 it was adopted by the District of Columbia as its official flower.

AS CONFIRMED BY THE IMMORTAL BARD, A ROSE BY ANY OTHER NAME WOULD SMELL AS SWEET.

MARGARET MERRIL

What lady would not be delighted to have a rose named for her? 'Margaret Merril' is very much a lady's rose, delicate blush in colour, sweetly fragrant and with a pleasing ruffled shape to the outer petals.

English breeder Jack Harkness was asked to provide a rose for the makers of the beauty preparation Oil of Ulay. To call it 'Oil of Ulay' was considered unacceptable. At the company's suggestion it was named for their Beauty Counsellor and so it became known as Margaret Merril'.

Budwood had been sent to Harkness' agents overseas, and one day a call came from Switzerland. 'We need to register the name, so please ask Mrs Merril to write giving her consent.' A call to Oil of Ulay disclosed that Margaret Merril was a fictitious lady used for their letters of advice.

Since then, three ladies called Margaret Merril have come forward, one from New York and two from Britain. They are all delighted to grow the rose and enjoy it as their own. Indeed 'Margaret Merril' has admirers in many lands, being voted best floribunda in the RINZ trial at Auckland in 1991, and James Mason Gold Medal winner in the UK in 1990 as the rose that has given most pleasure over the past 15 years.

KNOWN THROUGHOUT THE WORLD FOR PROMOTING ROSES, ESTHER GELDENHUYS' ROSE IS A MAGNIFICENT PINK.

CHEROKEE

A white rose grows wild in China, clambering up to 30 ft (10 m) or more by hills and streams. The Chinese give it the name 'Golden Cherry' after its hips, and it is portrayed in a herbal of 1406. Around 1700 it was brought to Europe, and thence to North America. This lovely variety flourished so well in the Atlantic seaboard states that it was soon growing almost everywhere, and today this much-loved Chinese immigrant is the adopted emblem of the state of Georgia.

A BOWL OF GLORIOUS ESTHER GELDENHUYS ROSES ADORN AN ELEGANT DINING ROOM.

LIVING WITH ROSES

*For nothing liken me might more
Than dwelling by the Rose aye
And then never to pass away.*

GEOFFREY CHAUCER (1340–1400)

ART

The earliest known illustration of a rose was discovered by Sir Arthur Evans in his excavation of the Minoan palace at Knossos on the island of Crete. Only one flower with the original colour remains, others having been re-painted. It is pink and probably depicts *R. gallica* 3,500 years ago. Another famous rose in art was actually called 'Rose des Peintres', the rose of the painters. This was the petal-packed Centifolia rose, darling of Dutch and

AMID A PROFUSION OF COLOUR, ROSES MAKE THE FINAL STATEMENT OF BEAUTY.

Flemish masters of the 17th century. They also favoured the white *R. alba*, and both were usually portrayed in full-blown beauty.

During the Renaissance period, the Virgin Mary, Mother of Christ, was often depicted in old paintings surrounded by roses or standing in a rose garden, and in some she was even garlanded with roses. And so the rose became Mary's own flower

All through history and throughout the world, roses have been carved and sculpted in temples and churches, painted on porcelain and silk, and roses are still extremely popular on furnishings and clothing fabrics, and china. In galleries or shops which sell works of art, one is sure to come across prints with the name Redouté written on their lower edge. These are the works of Pierre Joseph Redouté, who was commissioned to paint the amazing collection of roses in the garden at Malmaison which was founded by Empress Josephine. With a touch of genius, he brought to his pictures all the satin texture, delicate colour and translucence of the roses he loved to paint. A Redouté print is still distinctive, for no else has been able to paint roses quite as he did.

SINCE TIME IMMEMORIAL, ROSES HAVE BEEN THE FAVOURED SUBJECT OF POETS AND WRITERS ALIKE.

THE CHURCH

The rose was originally regarded as something heathen and pagan by the early Christians, but through the centuries it gradually gained favour with the Church, and its

*The wilderness and the solitary place
shall be glad for them:
and the desert shall rejoice,
and blossom as the rose.*

ISAIAH 35:1

DEEP RED VELVET BLOOMS CARRIED ON LONG STEMS MAKE BLACK MADONNA IDEAL FOR THE VASE.

A MULTITUDE OF ROSES HELP TURN THIS MARVELLOUS GARDEN INTO A FLORAL WONDERLAND.

spectacular stained glass windows are to be found in the famous Gothic cathedral, Notre-Dame. These windows date back to the thirteenth century.

Legend has it that Theophilus, the secretary of the judges who condemned Dorothea to death, scornfully told her as she was led to her execution that she should send him fruit and roses when she reached Paradise. The evening after Dorothea's execution, as Theophilus was sitting down to dinner, an angel appeared to him and his guests and offered him a basket of apples and roses, saying 'From Dorothea, in Paradise'. The heathen Theophilus was thus converted to Christianity.

And when St Bernadette saw Our Lady of The Grottos at Lourdes, she described the apparition as a 'beautiful lady with roses at her feet' who was revealed from behind a curtain of roses.

Other saints associated with roses are St Elizabeth of

enchanting blooms became prominent in Christian festivals as ornamentation, and it was even dedicated to Mary as her own flower.

In India, rosaries were made of compressed rose petals, and in Europe rose hips were used. Today, you may still find rosaries of rosewood, but glass, and even plastic, is more common.

France, the home of many magnificent roses, is also famous for its glorious cathedrals, with their stained glass and superb rose windows. Especially beautiful are those of Chartres and Notre-Dame de Paris. Probably the most

ROSES, OFTEN DEPICTED IN STAINED GLASS, ADORN A GLORIOUS OLD, STONE CHURCH.

Portugal and St Rose of Viterbo who carry roses in their hands, and St Rosalia, St Angelus and St Victoria who wear the blooms around their heads.

Even to this day, Rose Sunday is celebrated on the fourth Sunday in Lent, when traditionally popes have blessed a Golden Rose, dipped it in balsam, sprinkled it with holy water and then burned it. Julius II and Leo X both sent a papal rose to young Henry VIII of England, in the years before his breach with Rome.

The Rosary, used by Catholics to keep count of their repetitions of prayers, is said to be named after the chaplet of beads perfumed with roses given by the Virgin Mary to St Dominic, but this cannot be historically true as the term 'rosary' was already common in 1100 AD, centuries before the emergence of the young saint. Some claim that the first string of prayer beads was made of rosewood, while others maintain it takes its name from the 'Mystical Rose', one of the titles of the Mother of Christ.

From the beginning of the ninth century, the Pope pre-

sented a Golden Rose to women of peerless virtue, but the Christian Church, and Catholicism in particular, was not the only advocate in the spirituality of the rose. The rose, like the marigold and the lotus, plays an important part in divine worship in many Eastern religions.

An old church tradition is still continued at Abbotts Ann in England where rose wreaths of paper or linen are displayed, commemorating virgins of the parish. The oldest surviving ones are from the 18th century, and the most recent is dated 1973.

THE CHARMING OLD-FASHIONED LOOK OF ST ANDREWS EARNED IT A GOLD MEDAL AT THE GENEVA TRIALS.

MEDICINE

John Lindley, the renowned botanist and first professor of botany at the University of London, wrote that 'a pharmacopoeia should be made of roses alone'. This is an indication of the respect conferred upon the medicinal qualities of roses throughout the ages. Even during the Dark Ages, when the love of beautiful things seemingly disappeared, monasteries continued to cultivate roses. But the monks grew them not for their beauty, but for their medicinal values – and these were seemingly endless.

For hundreds of years, roses were used to allay pain and to relieve all kinds of human sufferings. Rosewater was taken for trembling and shaking, and a decoction of rose petals strengthened the heart and refreshed the spirit. Indigestion, debility, throat and skin infections, and inflammation of the eyes were all relieved by rose petals or rosewater. A plaster of rose petals alleviated inflammation of the stomach, as well as benefitting retentive faculties. They stimulated the appetite, and aided sleep. So said John Parkinson, grower of roses in the sixteenth century.

WHEN IT FIRST APPEARED, SIMPLICITY, WITH ITS OPEN BLOOMS, WAS HAILED AS A PINK ICEBERG.

Rosa gallica officinalis, the Apothecary's rose, was grown in such vast quantities at the town of Provins that it became known as the rose of Provins, and the entire town was given over to the drying and processing of rose petals for the relief of innumerable ailments. Napoleon was a firm believer in their efficacy, and his armies were supplied with endless quantities. Apparently, petals boiled in white wine were efficacious for gunshot wounds.

ENTWINING OLD CAST IRON PILLARS, TAUSENDSCHON ACCOMPANIES COLOURFUL BOUGAINVILLEA AND PETUNIAS.

The rose distills a healing balm
The beating pulse of pain to calm.
PLINY (C. 61-113)

The ancient Greeks and Romans believed that ointment made from rose petals helped heal dog bites and, it is claimed, this is how the Dog Rose got its name.

Other ailments which could supposedly be treated through the healing powers of rosewater included aching joints, faintness, liver disorders and even headaches.

The Romans were the first to take roses into Brittain, but already the locals had come to know the value of the hips in their diet. The very first vitamin C supplement was, perhaps not surprisingly, extracted from rose hips and today rose hips are widely acknowledged as having a proportionately higher vitamin C content than blackcurrants and even oranges. They are a recognised preventative against scurvy and, during the Second World War, rose hips were collected and the valuable vitamin C extracted. In fact, roses were grown along the roads and in vacant fields in Germany especially for this very purpose.

THE BUDS OF SIXTH SENSE HAVE A GOLD UNDERSIDE WHICH OPEN TO DOUBLE FLOWERS OF CHERRY RED AND GOLD.

DEDICATED ENTHUSIASTS THROUGHOUT THE WORLD CONSIDER ROSE GROWING AN ART RATHER THAN A SCIENCE.

As in our own day, people in past times were seeking cures for baldness, and a recipe is given in the *Herball* of John Gerarde (1545-1612) which sounds like the last hope of the despairing. A rose gall, which looks like a mossy outgrowth on a stem and is in fact the nest of a gall-wasp grub, had to be crushed, mixed with grease from a bear, and massaged into the skin. The American breeder Gene Boerner, himself very thin on top, put roses on his head for a very different purpose. If a visitor said one of his roses did not smell, he would put it under his hat for a few minutes, then retrieve it. The humidity in such a confined space always served to activate the scent glands in the petals.

ROSES IN THE HOME

*From fairest creatures we desire
increase
That thereby beauty's rose might
never die.*

WILLIAM SHAKESPEARE (1564–1616)

Roses petals may be used in a variety of ways in the home. If they are to be eaten, the basal part of the petals, usually somewhat paler, should be nipped off as these have a bitter taste. Both for the pot and for decoration, it is better to remove this 'heel'.

Petals should be picked on a warm day and laid out in a dry place where they will not be attacked by mould. They should be turned occasionally and, when quite dry, stored in airtight jars.

If the petals are to be used for decoration, they should be picked when dry and then placed between the pages of a book or in a special press.

DRIED ROSES

Blooms may be dried by hanging them, head downwards, in a warm dry place, or by placing the separate heads into silica gel, a crystalline desiccant (drying agent) which is obtainable at most chemists and pharmacies. Place the flowers in the silica with their faces facing upwards, so that the crystals can be brushed gently between the petals. The flower should ideally be entirely covered for up to ten days. You will know that your roses have dried sufficiently when the blue or white silica crystals

PINK CLOUD MAKES A WELCOME GUEST AS IT PEERS OVER THE VERANDAH WALL.

ARTISTS WORKING ON CHINA DELIGHT IN THE NEVER-
ENDING VARIETY OF SHAPES AND COLOURS.

PRESSED FLOWERS

Rose petals are ideal for pressed flower pictures as there is a marvellous variety of shapes and sizes, and they keep their colour exceptionally well. Place them into position to make a pretty picture, and then gently glue each petal into place. When these pictures have been framed, paint or dust the backing paper with insecticide to prevent infiltration by small insects.

The petals can also be used to decorate candles. Having made your candle, glue the flowers into position and then, holding the candle by its wick, dip it into a saucepan of warmed wax. Then take it out as quickly as possible so that a thin film of wax is left covering the flowers.

Bookmarks and greeting cards are appreciated so much more if they are made at home. And they can be so much prettier too if they are decorated with rose petals. Using a clear glue, attach the petals to a piece of stiff card and then cover it with self-adhesive film available from most craft shops.

have turned pink. Remove the blooms immediately or they will become even more brittle than they are already. Some people like to spray the dried flowers with lacquer, but remember that they are extremely fragile and should be handled very gently.

Fine sand, or a mixture of sand and borax, can be used instead of silica gel, but remember to remove all the leaves and thorns before drying, especially if you intend to hang your roses out to dry. To make the stems firm, push a length of wire up through the calyx and make a loop within the flower to hold it in position. This should prevent the flower from falling while drying. It may also be a good idea to cut each stem a different length so that the blooms do not touch each other. All these methods produce equally successful results and your roses should look remarkably like fresh blooms.

POTPOURRI

Potpourri is an age-old way of bringing the scents of the garden into the home, and no flower is more suitable for this purpose than the rose. Its petals, above all else, have the ability to hold onto their fragrance long after their blooms have died.

The roses you have chosen for your potpourri should ideally be picked on a warm dry day, and the petals laid out on wire racks or newspaper to dry completely. Remember to turn the petals regularly to avoid mould forming, and, once they are dry, they may be stored in airtight jars, ready for processing.

There are many books which give recipes for different types of potpourri, and one simple recipe appears below. You will need:

POTPOURRI IN THE HOME CAPTURES THE ALLURING FRAGRANCE OF ROSES FROM THE GARDEN.

POTPOURRI

2 cups of dried rose petals
1 cup of dried petals of other garden flowers
4 teaspoons of orris root
2 teaspoons of ground cinnamon
1 teaspoon of rose oil
A handful of dried rosebuds
Dried leaves of lavender, rosemary and
*   lemon verbena*

Mix the dried rose petals with the petals of any other flowers which add colour, such as larkspurs, delphiniums, violas, or marigolds, and then add a few leaves of lavender, rosemary, and lemon verbena. Now add the orris root and ground cinnamon, and mix well. To this, add a few drops of rose oil, and toss well.

Store the petals in sealed jars and bags for a few weeks, after which they should be ready. Then add a few dried rosebuds for that final touch of elegance.

Although potpourri looks pretty in an open bowl, it will keep its fragrance better if it is kept in a sealed jar, and opened only occasionally. The potpourri you do not intend to use for a while should be stored in a dark, dry place. You could make small bags from pretty fabric, fill them with potpourri and place them in cupboards, or in a pouch with your tea cosy. Or fill a very small pillow with potpourri for a sick friend.

There are many variations of potpourri, including moist potpourri, and many flowers, such as cornflowers, borage and geraniums, which can be dried to enhance its appearance. Dried rose petals are also very popular as confetti at weddings.

THE BRIDAL MORN

And through the glass window
  shines the sun,
How should I love and I so young?
The bailey beareth the bell away:
The lily, the rose, the rose I lay.

ANONYMOUS

ROSEWATER

The Romans used rosewater to disguise evil smells and it has been a valued source of perfume since those very early days. Rosewater has also been used for cleansing, for medicine and in the kitchen, where it is still used to flavour sweets and desserts. Add a teaspoon of rosewater to a junket, or any moulded sweet.

Rosewater added to your Turkish Delight recipe will make all the difference to its flavour, and you can do the same with your favourite biscuit recipe by replacing three tablespoons of milk with rosewater. For a special treat, you could even add three tablespoons of rosewater to your pancake mixture.

A COURTYARD SPLASHED WITH COLOUR IS ENHANCED BY
ROSES CLIMBING THE PILLARS.

ROSE PERFUME

If you have enough heavily scented roses in your garden, you can make you own perfume. The process is rather long and could be quite tedious, but with a little patience, you will be delighted with the result. You will need:

ROSE PERFUME

2 litres (60 fl oz) water
1 teaspoon alum
450 grams (16 oz) suet
125 grams (4½ oz) lard
Fresh scented petals
Spirits of wine

A BREATHTAKING ARRAY OF PERFECT ROSES IS USED TO CREATE A FLORAL MASTERPIECE.

Dissolve the alum in the water and boil. Then add the fat and, once it has all dissolved, strain the mixture. Allow the fat to solidify, remove it from the liquid and then melt it once again. Once it is in liquid from, divide the fat into two shallow dishes, preferably with straight sides and allow it to solidify yet again.

Place the rose petals about 5 cm (2 in) deep, between the two slabs of fat. After about two days, remove the old petals and replace them with fresh petals. You may also like to add some other scented flowers.

Continue with this process until you run out of petals, and then dissolve the fat in equal quantities of spirits of wine and store it in a screw-top container. The liquid should be shaken once a day for at least three months, after which the liquid should be strained once. You now have a perfume with your own personal touch.

ROSE HIP JELLY

Boil 1 kg (2 lb) of rose hips in one litre (32 fl oz) of water until the hips are soft. Then strain them through muslin and add a teaspoon of tartaric acid and 450 g (1 lb) of sugar to the liquid. Bring the mixture to the boil once again, and simmer until it sets.

ROSE PETAL JELLY

Similar in taste to rose hip jelly, rose petal jelly is made with rose petals. To add some colour, you should preferably use the petals of a dark red rose, or one of an equally vibrant hue. You will need:

ROSE PETAL JELLY

900 grams (2 lb) of
    cooking apples
2 cups (1 pint) of water
1 cup (8 oz) of sugar
Juice of small lemon
50 grams (2 oz) rose petals

ROSE HIP JELLY AND ROSE PETAL CONSERVE ARE A PERFECT
ACCOMPANIMENT FOR SCONES OR TOAST.

Chop the apples into slices and boil them in the water along with the lemon juice until they are soft. Then strain. Break up the petals with your fingers and add two teaspoons of sugar. Simmer the new mixture in 150 ml (4 fl oz) water for about 15 minutes and then strain.

Once you have done this, combine the two liquids and bring to the boil, adding the rest of the sugar. Stir to dissolve the sugar and bring to a rapid boil until setting point is reached.

ROSE PETAL CONSERVE

Although sweet conserves are usually made with whole pieces of fruit, you could try making a selection using only fresh rose petals. Ideally, they should be fragrant and striking red. You will need:

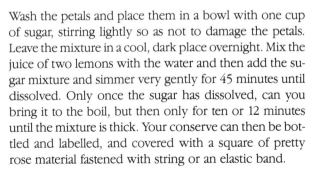

ROSE PETAL CONSERVE

1 cup rose petals
1 litre (40 fl oz) water
2 cups (1 lb)
    white sugar
2 lemons

Wash the petals and place them in a bowl with one cup of sugar, stirring lightly so as not to damage the petals. Leave the mixture in a cool, dark place overnight. Mix the juice of two lemons with the water and then add the sugar mixture and simmer very gently for 45 minutes until dissolved. Only once the sugar has dissolved, can you bring it to the boil, but then only for ten or 12 minutes until the mixture is thick. Your conserve can then be bottled and labelled, and covered with a square of pretty rose material fastened with string or an elastic band.

ROSE CORDIAL

For a refreshing drink on a hot summer day, there is little to beat a cool glass of rose cordial. You will need:

ROSE CORDIAL

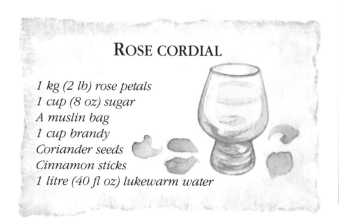

1 kg (2 lb) rose petals
1 cup (8 oz) sugar
A muslin bag
1 cup brandy
Coriander seeds
Cinnamon sticks
1 litre (40 fl oz) lukewarm water

Soak half the petals in water for the whole day. Then place them in the muslin bag and squeeze until all the water has been drained. Then put the rest of the petals into the water and leave for two days. Depending on how strong you prefer your cordial, you can repeat this process as often as you like. To this mixture, add the sugar and brandy, a few broken sticks of cinnamon and some coriander seeds. Then place the liquid in a covered container, leave for at least two weeks, strain and bottle.

THIS DELIGHTFUL CENTREPIECE IS CONFECTIONERY MADE ENTIRELY FROM CAKE ICING.

ROSE LEAF TEA

To make rose leaf tea, it is preferable to use the leaves, not the petals, of wild roses. Pour about two or three cups of boiling water over a handful or two of dried rose leaves, and leave for about ten minutes. Then strain and sweeten with honey.

CRYSTALLISED PETALS

For decorating that special cake or dessert, rose petals are a pretty addition. All you need to do is to whisk the white of an egg lightly so that it is not too stiff. Using a pair of tweezers, dip each petal into the mixture and then into a bowl of caster sugar. Lay them out to dry, and then use as needed. Crystallised rose petals look particularly beautiful on a wedding or christening cake.

FRESH PETALS

Many churches have forbidden the use of confetti at weddings, but will allow rose petals to be showered over the happy couple. The petals may be collected and dried as you would potpourri. Keep them in shallow boxes and sprinkle them occasionally with orris root powder. On the big day, place them in pretty baskets tied with ribbons and hand them to your guests.

Because they are edible, rose petals are a pretty decoration for cakes and puddings – scatter them liberally over desserts and sweets just before serving.

Rose petals can also be added to moulded puddings and ice cream, and sprinkle a generous handful of red rose petals over fruit salad.

Add a cupful to your next pudding in which cream and yoghurt are used. You could also put rose petals in your herbal tea, or freeze a few petals in ice blocks.

SET FOR TEA, THE TABLE HOLDS A CAKE DECORATED WITH SUGARED PETALS AND AN EPERGNE OF THE FAIRY.

When you are making apple jelly, turn some of it into rose petal jelly. Simply mix a cupful of rose petals with a dessertspoon of sugar, and break them up with a wooden spoon. Then add about a cup of water and simmer until soft. Strain well, and then add to the strained apple jelly.

For a tasty sauce, cook rose hips in water until they can be blended, then add a little lemon juice.

When selecting petals for use in the kitchen, avoid those which may have been sprayed. Bon appetit!

GLOSSARY

Anther
Pollen-bearing organ at the tip of the stamen.

Axil
The angle between the leaf stalk and the main stem where the axillary buds form.

Balling
After heavy rain, buds often cannot open because the wet outer petals tend to stick closely to one another.

Bare rooted plant
A plant which arrives from the nursery with its root exposed and not planted in a container.

Budding
A procedure whereby a live bud is taken from one plant and grafted onto another.

Bud union
The point on the stem at which a new bud has been inserted, and from which new growth will arise.

Callus
A mass of tissue which grows over a wounded surface such as a cut stem. Calluses also develop at the base of a cutting, from which a new root system will arise.

Calyx
The five sepals which enfold the young bud.

Cultivar
A strain deliberately produced by horticulturists.

Cutting
A part of a host plant, usually a stem, is removed and placed in a growing medium to produce a new plant which will entirely resemble the host plant.

Deadheading
The essential removal of dead flower heads, which will then encourage blooms to develop.

Dieback
Stems die back from the tip or from a pruning cut, usually caused by fungus or frost.

Disbudding
Side flower buds are removed, leaving the terminal bud free to develop. This is especially important if blooms are to be placed on show.

Dormant
During the cold months, and particularly in the colder parts of the country, growth slows down and almost stops. It is at this time that out of ground plants are lifted. (See also *Out of ground*)

Foliar feeding
The application of liquid fertilizer to foliage.

Hardiness
The natural ability of a plant to withstand frost.

Hip
The fruit of the rose.

Hybridisation
The creation of a new rose by taking the pollen from one rose and then applying it to another. (See also *Pollination*)

Inflorescence
The group of flowers at the end of the stem.

Internode
The part of the stem situated between two leaves.

Lateral
A side shoot growing from the main stem.

Leaching
The removal of nutrients from the soil by water.

Moss
Some roses have a coating of sticky outgrowths commonly known as 'moss'.

Mulch
The application to the surface soil of any material, normally organic, to retain moisture and to keep the soil cool.

Out of ground
During winter, when plants are dormant, they are lifted out of the ground, and sent to buyers with their roots virtually free of soil.
   (See also *Dormant*)

pH
A scale by which acidity and alkalinity is measured, with 7 as neutral, lower numbers as acid and up to 14 as alkaline.

Pistil
This consists of the flower's stigma, style and ovary.

Pollination
The transfer of pollen from the anther (male organ) of one flower to the stigma (female organ) of another so that seeds may form.
   (See also *Hybridisation*)

Pruning
The removal of old and weak wood, and the cutting back of existing stems to encourage fresh, new growth.

Quartered roses
The petals of many of the old roses are divided into four very distinctive parts.

Remontant
Repeat flowering. This means that the plant has more than one blooming during a season.

Scion
The bud or stem of a variety to be propagated, which is budded or grafted onto a stock.

Sepals
The five segments which form the calyx of the flower.

Species
A species rose is one which produces seeds which will give rise to plants and flowers identical to itself. All wild roses are species.

Sport
Occasionally, a plant will give rise to a stem which bears flowers different from others on the plant.

Stock
A species of rose onto which another is budded.

Sucker
A new stem which arises from the rootstock, below the bud union, which should then be removed.

Systemic
A systemic spray is one which is absorbed into the plant's system.

INDEX